The Thing of it is…

End Time Deception is here

To Woody! Shalom! Michael

Index added, June, 2018

Because of the dynamic nature of the Internet, any web addresses or links contained in this book may have changed since publication and may no longer be valid.

ISBN-13: 978-1974672813
ISBN- 10: 1974672816

Createspace Independent Publishing

Print information available on the last page.

Printed in the United States of America

In memory of Toni Lynn Kihntopf

If you keep repeating a lie long enough, the people listening will eventually believe it is true.

End Time Deception is Here strikes an eye-opening chord in today's sleepy religious environment. As a non-Jewish believer in Yeshua, I found this book to be a bold warning and wakeup call as he reveals the "Anti-Messiah" spirit that has been powerfully woven by the enemy into today's Western culture and into most denominations. It's a fascinating must-read, revealing key deceptions affecting and challenging both the believer and the Church today.

Steve Newton
President/CEO
Newton Media

There is information in this book that many Christians may have not considered or even been aware of. Dr. Reilly's scholarship and knowledge of the Hebrew Scripture and culture is considerable. This book raises questions which call all Believers to review their attitudes and opinions and to prayerfully address them. Once you read it, then you can decide.

Rev. Joseph McCauley
Founder Redemption and Triumph Ministries

Jeremiah 2:13

"for my people have committed two evils: they have forsaken me, the fountain of living waters, and hewed out cisterns for themselves, broken cisterns that can hold no water." (ESV) [1]

1 (ESV) Scripture quotations are from The Holy Bible, English Standard Version® (ESV®), copyright © 2001 by Crossway, a publishing ministry of Good News Publishers. Used by permission. All rights reserved.

Many read the Scriptures simply to reinforce their current beliefs. Although they read the entire Bible, their mind only sees certain doctrines. Instead of believing in what they read, they merely read what they already believe. Rarely do they find new truths in the Word. Baptists see from their perspective, Pentecostals and charismatics each have theirs, while Catholics and other denominations often have a completely different emphasis...When they are fully indoctrinated, their minds have been immersed into a pool of teaching that leaves them more conformed to the image of their sect than to the likeness of Christ. [2]

2 Francis Frangipane, *Holiness, Truth and the Presence of God*: (Cedar Rapids, IA: Arrow Publications, 1986), 56.

"Jesus draws a striking contrast [between] those who obey and those who disobey his instruction. Not only false teachers and false professors [are] in danger of eternal condemnation at judgement, but also another larger class, those who are hearers but not doers of the word…The doing of his word, the acting upon them, implies faith. Works is the evidence of faith".[3]

3 Rev. George W. Clark, *Notes on Matthew*, (Sheldon & Company: Philadelphia, PA, 1870), 105.

James 2:14, 17

14 What good is it, my brothers, if someone says he has faith but does not have works? Can that faith save him? (ESV)

17 So also faith by itself, if it does not have works, is dead." (ESV)

To sense the presence of God in the Bible, one must learn *to be present* to God in the Bible...The Bible is the frontier of the spirit where we must move and live in order to discover and to explore. It is open to him who gives himself to it, who lives with it intimately...*It is the Bible that enables us to know the Bible.* It is through the Bible that we discover what is in the Bible. Unless we are confronted with the word, unless we continue our dialogue with the prophets, unless we respond, the Bible ceases to be Scripture.[4]

4 Abraham J. Heschel, *Between God and Man* (New York, NY: Free Press Paperbacks, 1997), 243.

As we advance through the centuries, light and life begin to decrease in the Church. Why? Because the torch of the Scripture begins to grow dim and because the deceitful light of human authorities begins to replace it.[5]

Seeing the Bible through the eyes of an ancient reader requires shedding the filters of our traditions and presumptions...We view the Bible through the lens of what we know and what's familiar....Our traditions, however honorable, are not intrinsic to the Bible. They are systems we invent to organize the bible. They are artificial. They are *filters*.[6]

---

5 Quoted by Alfred Kuen in *I Will Build My Church*, translated by Ruby Linblad (Chicago: Moody, 1971), 27.

6 Michael S. Heiser, *The Unseen Realm*, (Lexham Press: Bellingham, WA, 2015), 13, 15, 17.

CONTENTS

INTRODUCTION

From the Author

1 John 2:18

"Children, it is the last hour, and as you have heard that antichrist is coming, so now *many antichrists have come*. Therefore we know that it is the last hour." (ESV, italics added)

What you are writing is a message that needs to be heard and taught over and over again. It is for that reason that I encourage you to write and teach this every chance you get! You write with much passion and this is very personal to you. As a reader I appreciate that.

Pastor Kyle Truman
Hope Fellowship

When I read passages like the one in 1 John 2:18, I have more questions than answers. Until I began the journey of doing the research for this book, for the most part, I looked to the future for antichrist and the great deception of the end times. *That has all changed.*

In First John 2:18, John confirms a fact that is already known to his readers; "many antichrists have come." Apparently John and his readers were very aware that there were individuals that were openly opposed to the Messiah; that this was not a new situation for them.

Then John goes on to say that "as you have heard ...antichrist is coming." The CJB translation states that "an Anti-Messiah is coming."[7] We should use caution about an Anti-Messiah (synonymous with antichrist). Why? At the writing of John's epistle, this foreboding evil was soon to come and it would overshadow the evil work of the "many antichrists" that were already at work. The seriousness is contained in John's last few words: "Therefore we know that it is the last hour."

Stop right here. Within the community of believers of the first century, the Enemy of God had already infiltrated the body of believers with "many antichrists." Add a couple thousand years, along with the establishment of the foretold Anti-Messiah, and where does this find us today?

Currently, we are all very aware that a terrorist can easily blend into one of our communities without being noticed. It is safe to assume that "many antichrists" are working in our churches doing their evil deeds right under our noses. These antichrists are so intermingled among us that we may not notice them or their true intent. Some antichrists are in positions of authority in our local churches.

In addition to these antichrists, John speaks that an antichrist (Anti-Messiah) is coming. The arrival of this evil "entity" is similar, yet far different and more destructive than the antichrists (an evil *entity* verses evil *individuals*). Antichrists are individuals that are controlled by demonic powers of darkness. However, Anti-Messiah seems to be, not

---

[7] (CBJ) *The Complete Jewish Bible*, Copyright © 1998 by David H. Stern and is published by Jewish New Testament Publications, Inc. All rights reserved. Used by permission.

a person, but perhaps an organization or governmental entity. Like the individual antichrists, Anti-Messiah may be difficult to identify.

It seems an obvious conclusion that antichrists are people claiming to be one of us, a Christian. The situation with the entity called Anti-Messiah is far more powerful than a single person. However, this entity, this Anti-Messiah, is not the Anti-Christ of Revelation 12-13.

The Scriptures informs us that there are:

(1) *many* antichrists (and deceivers; see 2 John 1:7),
(2) *an* Anti-Christ or Anti-Messiah (1 John 2:18), and
(3) *the* Anti-Christ (Revelation 12-13).

The "antichrists/deceivers" of 2 John 1:7 are individuals. The "Anti-Messiah" of 1 John 2:18 is a governmental or religious entity. "The Anti-Christ" found in John's Revelation is unique unto itself.

I have read that there are approximately 33,000 to 38,000 Protestant denominations in the world, which is an outrageous number.[8] Even if the actual number was a tenth of the highest estimate, it would still be an absurd number of separate denominations, if in fact we are all followers of "the Way" (Acts 9:2; 19:9, 23; 22:4; 24:14, 22).

8 http://blogforthelordjesuscurrentevents.com/2012/03/29/how-many-christian-denominations-are-there/, accessed July 13, 2017. Although there are others that support these large numbers of denominations (e.g., World Christian Encyclopedia or The Center for the Study of Global Christianity). I should note that these denominations may only be separate organizations or even independent churches and not necessarily separate beliefs.

I think that the concept of "denominations" is only found in the *Book of Second Opinions.*[9] If we were to inquire of each of these denominations, they would most likely defend their rationale for being a "separate" Christian denomination. Unfortunately, regardless of the rationale used, chances are good that pride, division and corporate disunity are their byproducts.

In spite of these denominations lacking a clear biblical validation, they continually divide and multiply as more and more denominations are birthed. In my opinion they have been easy pray for Anti-Messiah.

The deceptive force of the Enemy has masterfully transcended the denominational differences with such ease that, to me, it is extremely sobering. The evil work of Anti-Messiah is so powerful and misleading that it actually encompasses almost all denominations (in a demonic way) as unsuspecting Christians are seduced by the falsehood that has engulfed them.

The expression: "If you keep repeating a lie long enough; people will believe it is the truth," sums up the strategy that Anti-Messiah has propagated among the Western Christian world with great success!

I should note here that Anti-Messiah has redefined and manipulated what "biblical truth" is. This entity has not openly thrown out the core teachings of the Bible. Anti-Messiah has taken a glass of

9 *The Book of Second Opinions*, of course, is not an actual book in the Bible. It is a person's opinion that is not fully supported by the Bible, but often believed to be as important as God's Word. Religious traditions made by men fall under the umbrella of *Second Opinions*.

pure water and added a few drops of his poison to the water. Yes, biblical truth – the water – is there, but it is polluted with the poison. To drink from this glass may lead you to your death; eternal separation from the true Messiah.

My concern at this time is not with "antichrists" (2 John 1:7) or "the Anti-Christ" (Revelation 12-13). Rather, my focus is on Anti-Messiah as a possible religious institution, a governing body and/or a religious milieu through which false and deceptive doctrine and attitudes are forged and later propagated throughout Christendom.

For the most part, the work of Anti-Messiah seems to be isolated to the Church in the Western world and the nations that we have influenced.

> Matthew 7:15-20
>
> 15 "Beware of false prophets, who come to you in sheep's clothing but inwardly are ravenous wolves. 16 You will recognize them by their fruits. Are grapes gathered from thornbushes, or figs from thistles? 17 So, every healthy tree bears good fruit, but the diseased tree bears bad fruit. 18 A healthy tree cannot bear bad fruit, nor can a diseased tree bear good fruit. 19 Every tree that does not bear good fruit is cut down and thrown into the fire. 20 Thus you will recognize them by their fruits. (ESV)[10]

---

[10] ESV - Scripture quotations are from *The Holy Bible, English Standard Version®* (ESV®), copyright © 2001 by Crossway, a publishing ministry of Good News Publishers. Used by permission. All rights reserved.

The LORD has told us that the true nature of an individual, that is in reality an antichrist, may be easily identified by looking at their "fruits." In contrast, a "Christian" religious body that operates as Anti-Messiah may not be so easily detected.

The depth of deception transcends hundreds of years and has been meticulously stitched into the very fabric of the Western Church culture in which it operates.

Allow me to set the stage for you by discussing the concept of a worldview. A worldview refers to "a comprehensive conception of the world from a specific standpoint."[11] (See *Appendix A* in the back of this book for more about *A Biblical Worldview*.) In other words, who you are right now, theologically, culturally, ethnically, communally, and the degree of unconfessed sin that exists in your life *all funnel down to the precise point* that you view, interpret, understand and evaluate the rest of the world. This spans from your neighbors to the ends of the earth.

> 1 John 2:18
> "Children, it is the last hour, and as you have heard that antichrist is coming, so now many antichrists have come. Therefore we know that it is the last hour." (NRSV) [12]

---

11 https://www.merriam-webster.com/dictionary/worldview, accessed October 19, 2017.

12 (NRSV) *New Revised Standard Version Bible*, copyright © 1989 the Division of Christian Education of the National Council of the Churches of Christ in the United States of America. Used by permission. All rights reserved.

What I have come to understand is that the "last hour" John speaks about (1 John 2:18) was unfolding even in his day at the end of the first century.

John gave us a prophetic warning that antichrist (Anti-Messiah) was coming. Although it would take a few years to become powerful, the forces of evil (this Anti-Messiah) were unleashing a deception that most every Christian in our Western world fails to notice. Why? Like me, they were deceived about what Anti-Messiah would look like!

In a biblical reality, the Enemy of God's people operates and attacks from a vulnerable position. Our Enemy is no match for our God. Therefore, to be successful, our Enemy uses a military strategy that focuses more on asymmetric[13] warfare of deception than conventional methods. Matthew did say that "false prophets" would come into our gatherings. These false prophets have one purpose and that purpose is to deceive us! Anti-Messiah has one purpose: To deceive us!

Now, if you were to purchase a car that you think is a lemon,[14] would you only ask the dealer that sold you the car or would you go to

---

13 "Asymmetric warfare that is between opposing forces which differ greatly in military power and that typically involves the use of unconventional weapons and tactics (such as those associated with guerrilla warfare and terrorist attacks)." Source: https://www.merriam-webster.com/dictionary/asymmetric%20warfare, accessed November 16, 2017.

14 In Virginia, according to DMV, "To be a lemon, your vehicle must meet one of the following qualifications: Have unsuccessfully undergone 3 attempts at repair. Had 1 attempt at repair of a serious safety defect. Have been out of service for at least 30 days. Your vehicle will legally qualify as a lemon if any of these happened within the first 18 months of ownership by the first owner or lessee. https://www.dmv.org/va-virginia/automotive-law/lemon-law.php, accessed October 19, 2017.

a trusted mechanic? (I hope you go to the trusted mechanic.) Likewise with the topic at hand: Go to the final authority, which is the Bible.

As we look for evidence of the presence of Anti-Messiah, if we mistakenly look for a person, we will never notice the covert force of evil that has shrouded Western Christendom.

The topic of *End Time Deception* is one that is not new in the sense that discussions about the End Times are very popular. My concern is that the deception that is associated with the End Times is already here. Actually, it has been here for over sixteen hundred years! Many of us living in the Western World have already been seduced.

From what I can tell, the Eastern Christian World, fortunately, has been spared thus far. This is evident in that most of the effective evangelism today is taking place in countries like India, China, and the Muslim world. The believers in the East are willing to pay, and are paying, a steep price to reach the lost. We in the West, well, just take a look around at the spiritual health of the average believer and his or her biblical knowledge. You may also look at the status of the average local church on a congregational level.

Are you currently living as a Great Commission Christian?[15] As the expression goes, the proof is in the pudding: *End Time Deception* is here.

---

15 A Great Commission Christian is a believer who knows who he or she is in Christ. The idea of the priesthood of all Believers is not a concept, but a reality. This person has life-style knowledge of the Word of God. They not only know the Great Commission mandate, but they have built their lives around fulfilling it.

We may have heard that Anti-Messiah will deny the Father, Son and the Holy Spirit. If Anti-Messiah's military strategy is asymmetric warfare, then, perhaps, it will not overtly deny the Father, Son and Holy Spirit.

The entity or organization referred to in this book as *Anti-Messiah* will seek to dilute the truth found in the whole Bible.

Keep in mind that I am not referring to an individual deceiver or the Anti-Christ of John's Revelation. My focus is the Anti-Christ or Anti-Messiah of 1 John 2:18.

Anti-Messiah will seek to usurp the authority that rightfully belongs to God. Instead of God defining what it means to live a godly life, Anti-Messiah creates a "standard" that feels right, in that it agrees with our un-redeemed humanity. (An asymmetric warfare strategy fits better into the prophetic words about deception as mentioned in Matthew 24:24.)

I truly desire that each of us will be careful to study the Bible for what it says, and then do what the Bible tells us to do.

Let us make sure to have the entire Word of God as our foundation for life and service to the LORD. I am not expressing hyperbole in saying that this topic is clearly not for the average church-goer that is on a milk diet.

One pastor, and a good friend, cautioned me that this book would be difficult for an uneducated person or average layman to follow if I used language that the layman was unfamiliar with. This is most tragic. Why? For a person who regularly attends weekly services at a typical local church and NOT to understand the terminology and other biblical concepts in this book just proves the point of this book - We have been deceived and lulled to sleep.

> 1 Corinthians 3:2
> "I fed you with milk, *not solid food*, for you were not ready for solid food. *Even now you are still not ready*, (NRSV, italics added).

I wish this was not the case. However, aspects of this teaching have the potential of turning your Western theological world on its head. In other words, wreaking havoc on your current worldview. (See *Appendix A* for info about a biblical worldview.)

Those who are familiar with me and my teaching already understand that my overarching focus and concern is for every lover of God, every true believer, every born-again Christian to:

- ❑ Read the Bible for what it says; not what one may think or believe it says.
- ❑ To be followers of The Way and not only believing a few biblical facts.
- ❑ Obey what the Father tells you to do in His Word.

- I do not want you to seek to only *be a disciple* of the Messiah Yeshua[16] (Jesus), but to become a Great Commission Christian by *making disciples.*

I asked a good friend to read over a draft version of this book. Below is his response after reading it.

> This book will do more than shake a Christian to their very core. It will force the reader to look into their own life and ask the question, "Have I too been deceived?" In order for us to move forward, we must first "unlearn" some of what we have been taught about the Church and about the precepts of Christianity. I feel as though my very soul has been sandblasted of all that I once thought I knew or had learned.
>
> The historical Catholic church's influence on humankind, and more importantly, on the very fabric of our Christian beliefs, shows that a mana[17] type strategy is at work. The facts don't lie. The institutional Church has seized power that belongs to God alone. The Sabbath (Saturday) changed to Sunday to honor the sun god. The very arrangement of the Bible was changed. We find ourselves "going along in order to get along." Finally, we have anti-Semitism, the hatred of Jews worldwide, and replacement theology.

16 Yeshua was a common alternative form of the name "Yehoshuah" (Joshua) in later books of the Hebrew Bible and among Jews of the Second Temple period. Yeshua means "salvation" in Hebrew. It was also the most common form of the name Jesus and corresponds to the Greek spelling Iesous, from which, through the Latin Iesus, comes the English spelling Jesus. Source: David Stern, *Jewish New Testament Commentary*: (Clarksville, Maryland: Jewish New Testament Publications, 1992), 4,5

17 Mana - a generalized, supernatural force or power, which may be concentrated in objects or persons.

The evidence given by the author can be found throughout the Bible, both in the Old and New Testaments. The meat that has been placed before the reader is, in a sense, well done!

My prayer and advice to any and all readers of this book: Hang onto your seats; it's going to be a bittersweet ride through history to the present day. This is not milk; it is a seven course meal, come hungry.

Ronnie S. Bergholz

CHAPTER ONE

No Time for Recovery

Matthew 7:21-24
"Not *everyone who says to me, 'Lord, Lord,' will enter the kingdom of heaven, but the one who does the will of my Father* who is in heaven. On that day many will say to me, 'Lord, Lord, did we not prophesy in your name, and cast out demons in your name, and do many mighty works in your name?' And then will I declare to them, *'I never knew you; depart from me, you workers of lawlessness.'*
"Everyone then who hears these words of mine and does them will be like a wise man who built his house on the rock. (*italics added*)[18] (ESV)[19]

At some point in time, each of us has been deceived or misled; we may have even been lied to. This may have cost us a few dollars, perhaps a friendship or even something else very dear to us. Usually, given enough time and resource, we can recover from these types of deceptions. However, *End Time Deception* may have few options for recovery.

What goes through your mind when you read a passage like Matthew 7:21-24 quoted above?

---

18 The biblical context in which this passage was written reveals that "lawlessness" means that absence of law, absence of *Torah* (the teachings of the Bible).

19 Scripture quotations are from The Holy Bible, English Standard Version® (ESV®), copyright © 2001 by Crossway, a publishing ministry of Good News Publishers. Used by permission. All rights reserved.

If you are absolutely positive that you are NOT one of these "workers of lawlessness" and that you have NOT personally studied the Bible to know what is Truth, then, perhaps, you should be concerned!

In this passage in Matthew, Christ is saying that the Bible, the whole Bible, is our foundation; the foundation upon which we build our lives. If the foundation is wrong or weak, what will happen to what is built upon it?

The words, "Lord, Lord" are the words that many churchgoers say, yet simply saying these few words is NOT enough to secure one's eternal salvation. The people that Jesus is talking about are not pagans who have not heard the Gospel message. He is addressing professing Christians![20]

One may call the Messiah as the divine Lord and still NOT have a relationship with His Father YHWH [yeh-ho-vaw'].[21] Biblically, to ONLY say the right words *does not grant you salvation.*

Matthew 8

28 When he came to the other side, to the country of the Gadarenes, two demoniacs coming out of the tombs met him.

---

20 Read the story about Simon in Samaria in Acts 8 for a biblical case study that saying or believing the right things will not bring about salvation.

21 In the *Tanakh*, YHWH (or YHVH) is the personal name of God. When the written letters YHWH are read aloud by Jewish people, the word *Adonai* is spoken. YHWH (or YHVH) is the name of God that cannot be spoken. God's name as the tetragrammaton YHWH (or YHVH) is Yahweh. Tetragrammaton means "the four letters." It is composed of the Hebrew letters Yod, Heh, Vav, Heh (אֲדֹנָי). Although the actual phonetic sound of the four letters has been lost in time, at times we simply sound out 'yeh-ho-vaw' for LORD. In Luke 4:18, when Jesus quotes Isaiah 61:1, He states "The spirit of the Lord is upon me" Jesus is saying YHWH is upon Him.

> They were so fierce that no one could pass that way. 29
> Suddenly they shouted, *"What have you to do with us, Son of God?*
> Have you come here to torment us before the time?" 30 Now a
> large herd of swine was feeding at some distance from them. 31
> The demons begged him, "If you cast us out, send us into the
> herd of swine." (NRSV, italics added)

We need to realize that all demons know Christ as the Son of God. To only make a verbal profession about who Christ is puts you on par with a demon. What must occur is what demons cannot do: **We must hear His words *and* then do the Word.**

Many have told me throughout my life that I walk like my biological father. I have been told that I have mannerisms and facial expressions that he had. Why do I have behavior like my father? His DNA is in my physical body, therefore; there is clear cause-effect. Since the day when I made the Messiah the Lord of my life, I have been shaped by my heavenly Father, His Son, His Holy Spirit, and His Word. I guess I could say that God's DNA has also shaped my life profoundly; clear cause-effect.

So, you call yourself a Christian. You even go to church on Sunday. You read the Bible at times. Great! However, does your life reveal the relationship you claim to have with God the Father? Do others see the Word of God in the way you live your life and the words you speak? Do you live out the teachings of the Bible in the decisions that you make? If this is not the case, then, perhaps, there is a real possibility that He does not know you!

Regardless of what you have been taught or what you currently believe, the Bible is the ONLY and FINAL authority that should govern our lives. Matthew 7:24 is not listed as an option or as a take it or leave it command. "Everyone then who *hears these words* of mine ***and*** *does them* will be like a wise man who built his house on the rock" (ESV, italics and bold added).

> John 6:38
>
> For I came down from heaven, not to do mine own will, but the will of him that sent me. (KJV) [22]

The Messiah only did what the Father told Him to do. The Father has told us what to do in His Word.

Look again at the wording of Matthew 7:23, "And then will I declare to them, 'I never knew you; depart from me, you workers of lawlessness.'" The Greek word translated to the English "lawlessness" is *anomia. Anomia* means the "absence of law" which hebraically speaking means "absence of *Torah*."[23] (Note: Please study this footnote.

---

22 KJV - The Holy Bible, *The King James Version of the Bible* was originally published in 1611.

23 The word *Torah* may be new for you. The first mention of the Gospel is found in the *Torah*. Every believer in the first century, with very few exceptions, fully understood the meaning of this word, *Torah*. All of the truths presented in what is called The New Testament are found in either the *Torah* or the *Tanakh*. Remember the Bereans? (Acts 17:10-11) They validated the relevance of Paul's message by comparing what Paul taught against what was written in the *Torah* and/or the *Tanakh*. The word Scripture and Scriptures, which is found over 50 times in the New Testament, is referring to *Torah* and/or the *Tanakh*.

The word *Torah* means instruction or teaching. The *Torah* is full of instructions, statutes, laws, directives, and rules. Of which, most are directed to the Israelites, some to all ethnic groups. *(Continued on next page)*

Make sure that you know what the expression "absence of *Torah*" fully means before you continue.)

Grasp what is being conveyed in the text in Matthew 7. People may call the Messiah in a respectful way, Lord, yet not obey His Word; the teachings of the Bible. Only those who obey the teachings of the Bible will enter into the Kingdom of Heaven![24]

If saying a few words or mentally "agreeing" with a religious idea or concept was all that was required for salvation, then the Lord would not have added the condition about "doing" the Father's will. For that matter, God could have put the message on a post card and have done away with the Bible as we know it.

As we will understand later in this book, to think like the original readers of the Bible and to obey the Word is to "do" the Word. These are two sides of the same coin. This involves the whole person: body, soul and spirit.

The words of the *Torah* constitute what the rabbinic tradition calls the Written *Torah*. However, beginning around 400 BC, teachings emerged based in or connected to the *Torah*, but not literally evident in the text. This body of teaching is known as the Oral *Torah*, and rabbinic sources claim that it, too, was revealed at Sinai. *Halacha* is the "way" a descendant of Jacob is directed to behave, encompassing civil, criminal and religious law. *Halacha* per se begins with this "Oral *Torah*." (Source: https://www.myjewishlearning.com, accessed November 21, 2017.)

I should also note that *Halacha* is based upon Leviticus 19:2 "Speak to all the congregation of the people of Israel and say to them, You shall be holy, for I the LORD your God am holy" (ESV). (The Messiah quotes this verse in 1 Peter 1:16.) Therefore, *Halacha* provides practical advice as to how to live a holy life. It encompasses both the way to "go" and the way to "walk." This Jewish concept is reflected in many sermons in our non-Jewish local churches. The epistle of James in the New Testament echoes the heart of *Halacha*. James 1:22, "But be doers of the word, and not hearers only, deceiving yourselves" (ESV). James 2:17 "…faith by itself, if it is not accompanied by action, is dead" (NIV). To declare that *Torah* and *Halacha* are the "law" and are no longer relevant to Gentile believers, to a large degree, is to deny what the Messiah taught as well.

24 Obedience is not the cause of one's salvation **but the result** of being born-again.

This reality can be expressed this way: We know the Word **and** we do the Word. We should never have one without the other. To do so is to be a living lie, a hypocrite.

If those who proclaim, and really mean what they said, that the Father is the absolute authority in their lives, wouldn't we be doing the "will" of the "Father."

The will of the Father is not synonymous with doing the will of your pastor or following the traditions of your local church.

Question: Where do we find the will of the Father?

It does not matter what a person has said or done in God's name, or Jesus' name, or even in the name of the Holy Spirit, or the church's name, if it was not birthed from the fact that the Father (and His Son) is the Lord; the absolute owner of the person's life.

We are all too familiar with the "religion of Christianity" which is centered on the activities of a local church building. As we shall see, this is, in part, an effect of the *End Time Deception.*

What Matthew (7:21-24) addresses is the reality that God alone is the One that gives us, His followers, our marching orders. God's instructions are located in the entire Bible, Genesis to Revelation.

But wait, you may tell me that you are a "New Testament Christian and are no longer under the Law."

Could you grab a blank sheet of paper and write down what exactly is meant by expression "the Law." For your answer, please ONLY use what the Bible says and not what you may have heard. Afterwards, you may want to re-evaluate your position; "I am no longer under the Law." Why? The Bible makes it clear to the reader what will happen if anyone adds or takes away from His Word. You may very well be surprised at the degree of deception that has influenced you as you research your answer.

For clarification, the warning in Revelation 22:18-19 about adding or taking away from this book is specific to the prophecies found in the Book of Revelation. However, the principle provided in Revelation 22 is applicable to anyone who misrepresents any part of God's Word. A similar warning is given in Deuteronomy 4:1-2 and Proverbs 30:5-6 where God's Word cautions the hearer that they must listen **and** obey the Word (the commandments).

Once a Gentile man or woman has a relationship with the Father, through the finished work of the Son, the Messiah, and has been grafted into the true vine, we become part of Israel.[25] We must be careful to handle the Bible with care and reverence so as to not distort its message.

Let me comment about spiritual grafting.

> Romans 11:11-31
>
> 11 So I ask, have they stumbled so as to fall? By no means! But through their stumbling salvation has come to the Gentiles, so as to make Israel jealous. 12 Now if their stumbling means riches for the world, and if their defeat means riches for Gentiles, how much more will their full inclusion mean! 13 Now I am speaking to you Gentiles. Inasmuch then as I am an apostle to the Gentiles, I glorify my ministry 14 in order to

25 Not all Jews are part of biblical Israel. Although we may not know who is a true Israelite, the LORD does.

make my own people jealous, and thus save some of them. 15
For if their rejection is the reconciliation of the world, what will
their acceptance be but life from the dead! 16 *If the part of the
dough offered as first fruits is holy, then the whole batch is holy; and if the
root is holy, then the branches also are holy. 17 But if some of the branches
were broken off, and you, a wild olive shoot, were grafted in their place to
share the rich root of the olive tree, 18 do not boast over the branches. If
you do boast, remember that it is not you that support the root, but the root
that supports you.* 19 You will say, "Branches were broken off so
that I might be grafted in." 20 That is true. They were broken
off because of their unbelief, but you stand only through faith.
So do not become proud, but stand in awe. 21 *For if God did not
spare the natural branches, perhaps he will not spare you.* 22 Note then
the kindness and the severity of God: severity toward those
who have fallen, but God's kindness toward you, *provided you
continue in his kindness; otherwise you also will be cut off.* 23 And *even
those of Israel, if they do not persist in unbelief, will be grafted in, for God
has the power to graft them in again.* 24 For if you have been cut
from what is by nature a wild olive tree and grafted, contrary to
nature, into a cultivated olive tree, how much more will these
natural branches be grafted back into their own olive tree. 25
So that you may not claim to be wiser than you are, brothers
and sisters, *I want you to understand this mystery: a hardening has come
upon part of Israel, until the full number of the Gentiles has come in.* 26
And so *all Israel will be saved; as it is written*, "Out of Zion will
come the Deliverer; he will banish ungodliness from Jacob." 27

> *"And this is my covenant with them, when I take away their sins."* 28 *As regards the gospel they are enemies of God for your sake; but as regards election they are beloved, for the sake of their ancestors; 29 for the gifts and the calling of God are irrevocable.* 30 Just as you were once disobedient to God but have now received mercy because of their disobedience, 31 so they have now been disobedient in order that, by the mercy shown to you, they too may now receive mercy. (NRSV, italics added)

A complete teaching on this passage is a book unto itself. However, you may want to carefully re-read the italics once more. Be sure to read them in context. Only the unbelieving Jews are temporarily cut off, but not all Jews. Gentiles, like a wild olive tree, are grafted into the true olive tree; faithful Israel.

Two points: (1) **If** all of Israel[26] is currently cut off from God and the covenant with Abraham, Isaac, and Jacob is null and void, **then** the believing Gentiles are grafted into a dead tree! (2) After being grafted into the true Israel and when a Gentile believer states that he or she is not under the teachings of the Old Testament, he or she has believed a lie.

It makes no difference how educated a pastor is or how anointed he or she may be, God has no partners or co-authors in the writing of His Word. His Word and His Word alone is the Final Authority on any matter concerning Him or our salvation.

---

26 Throughout this book I refer to Israel as the collective body of people that have descended from Jacob.

The individuals that only serve God with their words and religious activities at "their church" may hear the words, "I never knew you; depart from me, you workers of lawlessness." We have to both "hear" the Word **and** "do" the Word.

CHAPTER TWO

What the Church Should Look Like

> Acts 9:2a
> And desired of him letters to Damascus to the synagogues, that if *he found any of this way*... (KJV, italics added)
>
> Acts 11:26
> And when he had found him, he brought him unto Antioch. And it came to pass, that a whole year they assembled themselves with the church, and taught much people. And *the disciples were called Christians first in Antioch.* (KJV, italics added)

What does the Bible tells us about the followers "of this way"? What is significate of their being called "Christians" in Acts 11:26? The attributes found in the Book of Acts are rarely witnessed in our Western local churches today. We, at times, expend a great amount of resources to re-create our perception of the Early Church; seldom with any true success.

If we are objectively honest with ourselves we look more like the Catholic Church, which we broke away from during the Reformation, than the example of the Christian community found in the Bible.[27]

27 Protestants originally broke away from the Roman Catholic Church. When I mention the Catholic Church I am mostly addressing the Catholic Church in an historical sense. I do not mean to offend any believers that identify with the Catholic Church today.

The Early Church was made up of the initial followers of the Messiah. If we were "doers" of the Word and not just pew sitters on Sunday, chances are good that we would look and live like the believers recorded in the Book of Acts.

Acts 11:15-26

15 As I began to speak, the Holy Spirit fell on them
just as on us at the beginning. 16 And I remembered
the word of the Lord, how he said, 'John baptized
with water, but you will be baptized with the Holy
Spirit.' 17 If then God gave the same gift to them as
he gave to us when we believed in the Lord Jesus
Christ, who was I that I could stand in God's way?"
18 When they heard these things they fell silent. And
they glorified God, saying, "Then to the Gentiles also
God has granted repentance that leads to life." 19
Now those who were scattered because of the
persecution that arose over Stephen traveled as far as
Phoenicia and Cyprus and Antioch, speaking the
word to no one except Jews. 20 But there were some
of them, men of Cyprus and Cyrene, who on coming
to Antioch spoke to the Hellenists also, preaching the
Lord Jesus. 21 And the hand of the Lord was with
them, and a great number who believed turned to the
Lord. 22 The report of this came to the ears of the
church in Jerusalem, and they sent Barnabas to
Antioch. 23 When he came and saw the grace of God,

he was glad, and he exhorted them all to remain faithful to the Lord with steadfast purpose, 24 for he was a good man, full of the Holy Spirit and of faith. And a great many people were added to the Lord. 25 So Barnabas went to Tarsus to look for Saul, 26 and when he had found him, he brought him to Antioch. For a whole year they met with the church and taught a great many people. And in Antioch the disciples were first called Christians. (ESV)

Acts 2:42-47

42 And they devoted themselves to the apostles' teaching and the fellowship, to the breaking of bread and the prayers. 43 And awe came upon every soul, and many wonders and signs were being done through the apostles. 44 And all who believed were together and had all things in common. 45 And they were selling their possessions and belongings and distributing the proceeds to all, as any had need. 46 And day by day, attending the temple together and breaking bread in their homes, they received their food with glad and generous hearts, 47 praising God and having favor with all the people. And the Lord added to their number day by day those who were being saved. (ESV)

Acts 4:32-35

Now the full number of those who believed were of one heart and soul, and no one said that any of the things that belonged to him was his own, but they had everything in common. 33 And with great power the apostles were giving their testimony to the resurrection of the Lord Jesus, and great grace was upon them all. 34 There was not a needy person among them, for as many as were owners of lands or houses sold them and brought the proceeds of what was sold 35 and laid it at the apostles' feet, and it was distributed to each as any had need. 36 Thus Joseph, who was also called by the apostles Barnabas (which means son of encouragement), a Levite, a native of Cyprus, 37 sold a field that belonged to him and brought the money and laid it at the apostles' feet. (ESV)

Acts 5:12-16
Now many signs and wonders were regularly done among the people by the hands of the apostles. And they were all together in Solomon's Portico. 13 None of the rest dared join them, but the people held them in high esteem. 14 And more than ever believers were added to the Lord, multitudes of both men and women, 15 so that they even carried out the sick into the streets and laid them on cots and mats, that as Peter came by at least his shadow might fall on some of them. 16 The people also gathered from the towns around Jerusalem, bringing the sick and those afflicted with unclean spirits, and they were all healed. (ESV)

In the space below write down the attributes or facts about the Early Church revealed in the previous Scriptures. (You are actually writing the contents of this chapter.)

1. ____

2. ____

3. ____

4. ____

5. ____

6. ____

7. ____

8. ____

9. ____

10. ____

11. ____

12. ____

13. ____

14. ____

15. ____

16. ____

17. ____

18. ____

19. ____

20. ____

(Go to *Appendix B* in the back of the book for possible answers.)

Please do not continue until you find at least twenty characteristics of the Early Church.

How does this list compare to the local church you attend?

CHAPTER THREE

Biblical vs Western Thinking: An Introduction

> The Hebrew language is consistent. Every letter has meaning…letters are built into root words, which have meaning…and root words are added to or combined to make other words. The words that are created carry the meaning of all that they are built upon. Just like the New Testament is built upon the old! And that art, that depth, that dimension of understanding…is lost in translation.[28]

This chapter could be titled, *Hebrew vs Greek Thinking.* However, since there is a fair amount of anti-Semitism within our Western churches, I selected *Biblical vs Western Thinking* as the title.

As we work our way through this material keep in mind that language and culture are closely related in that the words and expressions of a language may be "viewed as a verbal expression of culture. It is used to maintain and convey culture and cultural ties."[29]

From childhood to the present day, the values, traditions and customs of our Western World have shaped the way in which we think

---

[28] Seed of Abraham Ministries, Inc., Jennifer Ross, http://www.torahclass.com/archived-articles/429-anav-by-jennifer-ross, accessed September 24, 2017.

[29] http://www.lexiophiles.com/uncategorized/the-relationship-between-language-and-culture, accessed September 12, 2017.

and understand the world around us. In no small way, these forces extend to our understanding of the teachings of the Bible. Even when we hear a sermon or read the Bible we interpret what is said or read through our pre-existing worldview.

A living language, such as English, shifts and develops with each generation. As we have witnessed in the past few years, drastic changes occur during a single generation. In comparison to English, older languages like Hebrew and Aramaic are more static.

The King James Bible was written in English, a living language. It was not written in the original languages of the Bible nor was the original documents available to the translators. The Apostle Paul did not use a King James Bible as he would have used *Torah* and/or the *Tanakh*, and, perhaps, the *Septuagint.*[30] Therefore, to a modern reader, to varying degrees the original message is lost in translation.

---

30 The Septuagint is a Greek translation of the Hebrew Bible. It should be noted that this translation is not as reliable as the original Hebrew Bible. The details concerning the origin are blurred and it is difficult to know how much confidence we can give to the historical record concerning the Septuagint. There are several distinct changes that were made to the Bible. For example:

(1) In Proverbs 6:8b, after the Hebrew proverb of the ant, the Septuagint adds a Greek proverb of the bee. "Or go to the bee and learn how diligent she is, and how earnestly she is engaged in her work; whose labors kings and private men use for health, and she is desired and respected by all, though weak in body she is advanced by honoring wisdom."
(2) The original Septuagint translation of Daniel was thought to be too much of a paraphrase. *(Continued on next page.)*

When a person learns a second or third language, the learner is also introduced to the culture (or they should be!). Therefore, "culture has a crucial role in encoding and decoding messages" and supports the idea that "culture is at the heart of communication." In fact, it is the "body of knowledge of common beliefs, behaviors and values appear to be the factor to establish and interpret meaning in both verbal and nonverbal language."[31]

Idioms are fixed expressions that are typically used in a figurative sense. For example, in the sentence, *Exams are part of a carrot and stick method*, there are obviously no real carrots and sticks involved. The image is that of a donkey being encouraged to move forward by dangling a carrot in front of it or by hitting it with a stick. We can use this idiom to describe any event that involves more abstract rewards (the carrot) and threats (the stick). All languages are full of idioms, and native speakers use them spontaneously without even thinking about their figurative nature. Language learners generally find idioms hard to understand, and this is not surprising. For example, learners are often not sure

(3) A more famous and ultimately more significant example concerns the term "Red Sea." In Hebrew it is *yam suph* meaning "reed sea," a term which was used most famously to describe the body of water that the Israelites crossed as they escaped from Egypt. This body of water is often thought to be the lakes or salt water marshes at the northern end of the Gulf of Aqaba. The Septuagint, however, renders it *Erythra thalassa* meaning "Red Sea," and it is this translation that is used by the New Testament in Acts 7:36 and Hebrews 11:39. All English versions apart from the Jerusalem Bible stick with this tradition. (Source: http://www.biblearchaeology.org, accessed April 2, 2018.

31 Byram and Risager, *The Role of English language culture in the Omani language education system: An Ideological Perspective. Language, Culture and Curriculum*, 18 (3) 258-270. (1999, originally cited in Al-Issa, 2005 and in *Journal of Language Teaching and Research*, Vol. 4, No. 5, pp. 953-957, September 2013, www.academypublication.com/issues/past/jltr/vol04/05/07.pdf, accessed September 12, 2017.

what image the idiom is based on. If a native speaker proposes to show you the ropes and you are not familiar with this expression, you might not immediately understand that she is proposing to teach you how to do a certain job. It would help if you knew that the expression was originally used in the context of sailing, where an experienced sailor had to show a novice how to handle the ropes on a boat. *(Italics added for clarity)*[32]

Linguists used to believe that idioms were completely arbitrary: that is, you could not guess their meaning from the words they consist of. Consequently, teachers used to tell their students that the only way to master idioms was to learn them by heart. Fortunately, we now know that many idioms can be explained after all, and so they can be learned in systematic ways. Research tells us that when idioms are presented as non-arbitrary features of language, students find them much easier to understand and remember.[33]

Many idioms are derived from our general physical experiences. For example, the expressions hot under the collar, breathe fire, and let off steam all refer to being angry, and they do this through the image of anger as something hot inside us. This makes sense to us, because when people get angry they often get red in the face as a result of rising body temperature. Similarly, the figurative expressions lend someone a hand, try your hand at something, and have your hands tied all use the image of the hand to refer to performing an action. This also makes sense, because we know from everyday experience that most activities involve the use of our hands.[34]

---

32 http://www.macmillandictionaries.com/MED-Magazine/February2008/49-LA-Idioms.htm, accessed September 12, 2017.

33 Ibid.

34 Ibid.

Besides common idioms, in comparing Greek to Hebrew, Greeks viewed the world through "abstract thought" while Hebrews viewed the "world through the senses (concrete thought)." Allow me to use an example from Psalm 103:8, "The LORD is merciful and gracious, slow to anger, and plenteous in mercy" (KJV). Let's focus on the expression "slow to anger." The Hebrew word translated into the English word "anger" literally means "nose." When someone is very angry, and as his breathing increases, their "nostrils begin to flare." Therefore, a Hebrew sees anger as "the flaring of the nose (nostrils)." If the English translator had literally translated the Hebrew words "slow to nose," it just wouldn't make any sense to us.[35]

Although there are many examples, for clarity at this point, let's look at a couple of simple idioms. In the ESV, Philippians 3:2 has the expression "Look out for the dogs." Not the four-legged kind of dog, but beware of "gossipers and troublemakers."[36] A word study using *Strong's Exhaustive Concordance* does not make note of this idiom. Strong's #2965, for the Greek word *kuón* (or *kýōn*) is referenced, which (literally) means a dog, scavenging canine or (figuratively) a spiritual predator who feeds off others. The difference is significant in that "gossipers and troublemakers" are not exactly the same as a "spiritual predator who feeds off others."

---

35 http://ancient-hebrew.org/m/articles_thought.html accessed September 23, 2017.

36 George M. Lamsa, *Idioms in the Bible Explained* (Harper One: New York, 1985), 64, 62.

In the KJV, Romans 16:4 reads, "Who have for my life laid down their own necks" which means "Willing to work hard; to die for the truth." [37]

The cohesion of a given language and culture forces us, the Western reader of the Bible, to lay aside our familiar and usual cultural lens of our language and its cultural bent. After which, we then may look at the Scriptures with fresh eyes. As we do so, we need to use care in how we understand the terminologies and imperatives of the whole Bible. One way to express this is found in the following quote:

> Demonstrating our faith through obedience to God's word believing everything laid down in the *Torah* and prophets; we believe that the commandments are a guardrail to protect us, not a fence to restrict us.
>
> We do not teach that we follow *Torah* FOR salvation; we follow it **BECAUSE OF** our salvation and faith in its Author.[38] (italics and bold added)

In just over 300 years after Thomas Aquinas made intellectual reasoning the official position of the Catholic Church, which changed how we share our faith, René Descartes made his lasting impression upon the Western world. Descartes, a French philosopher, mathematician, and scientist, who has been called the father of modern western philosophy, drives a deeper wedge between Western/Greek and the ancient Hebrew mindset. (Descartes lived during the period known as the Reformation.) Where Thomas Aquinas propagated the

---

37 Ibid..

38 http://thewaybiblicalfellowship.com, accessed September 12, 2017.

concept of "systematic intellectual" and "philosophical theology"[39] in the study of the Bible and "articulated a philosophical rationale for the hierarchical order that the medieval [Catholic] Church embraced,"[40] Descartes gave us a new problem that greatly shifted how theologians interacted with the teachings of the Bible, as well as the operation of God's people.

Instead of using the approach that Hebrews had used for millennia, Descartes introduced Westerners to interpreting the world and the Word through the relationship of "spirit to matter, of mind to body, of God to creation." His renowned aphorism, "I think, therefore I am," gives primacy to one's intellect, "with a consequent devaluation of body, a dualism that would stamp the modern age, and that can be recognized as dividing the emotional from the rational, the individual from the community, the scientific from the artistic, (and) the pragmatic from the moral." [41] The concept of the separation of church and state is a byproduct of this dualism.

You may want to pause here for a moment. Descartes introduced Westerners to his aphorism, "I think, therefore I am." If a Westerner applies this concept to salvation, the results may lead to eternal damnation; all the while the lost person "thinks I am going to heaven" without a single biblical reference supporting what is believed.

Hebraic thinking is found in Proverbs 16:2, "All a person's ways seem pure to them, but motives are weighed by the LORD."

---

39 James Carroll, *Constantine's Sword* (Houghton Mifflin Company: New York, 2002), 301

40 Carroll, *Constantine's Sword*, 305

41 Carroll, *Constantine's Sword*, 408

What we do must be birthed from the Word of God. It is the Bible that is the energy and force within our biblical and godly "motives."

The underlying principal is that every command in the Bible requires *physical action* based upon the imperative. So, when I speak about biblical thinking (Hebraic thinking) verses Western or Greek thinking, picture physical action taking place as a direct result of the biblical imperative (Hebrew thinking) ***verses*** mental or philosophical action or contemplation as a result of the imperative. This is why Scriptures like 1 2:9-11 speaks volumes as to where a person is in their relationship with God.

> 1 John 2:9-11
>
> "The one who says he is in the Light and yet hates his brother is in the darkness until now. The one who loves his brother abides in the Light and there is no cause for stumbling in him. But *the one who hates his brother is in the darkness and walks in the darkness*, and does not know where he is going because the darkness has blinded his eyes." (NASB, italics added)[42]

This passage is why a true Christian CANNOT be a racist in any shape, fashion or form. This would include anti-Semitism. To love our brother *requires physical action*; doing something. Otherwise, the person is a liar and "*walks in the darkness*".

---

42 NASB - *New American Standard Bible* Copyright © 1960, 1962, 1963, 1968, 1971, 1972, 1973, 1975, 1977, 1995 by The Lockman Foundation, La Habra, Calif. All rights reserved.

The shift from studying the Bible from a Hebraic mindset to a Greek mindset began centuries before Thomas Aquinas made intellectual reasoning the official position of the Catholic Church and changed how we share our faith. That is, from "showing Christ in the way we live," to just "believing and saying" the right things. Even though we may not be Catholics, the "Mother" of all Protestants[43] is the Catholic Church. Her age old theological values are too often engrained into our current theologies.

Thomas Aquinas made reason and debate the norm. This is why we think we can *sell a lost person on why he or she should accept Christ as Savior.* This is not a biblical concept!

Why is it important that we understand the differences between biblical thinking verses Western/Greek thinking? Let's see why.

At best, if we only read and study the Bible through our Western/Greek paradigms by using the cultural and theological values of the Western world to interpret Scripture, in many cases, we may completely misread the biblical text. If this occurs, the door is opened for us to believe a lie and go into eternity separate from God the Father.

Although there are common mistakes in the linguistics, the issue that I am addressing goes far beyond simple linguistics (the morphology, syntax, phonetics, or the semantics of a language).[44]

---

43 Some Christian denominations do not claim to be either Catholic or Protestant. I will not get lost in the weeds of debate on this matter. For my purposes, Christians are either Protestants (the non-Catholics) or Catholics.

44 **Morphology** involves the forms of words, parts of speech (noun, verb, etc.), intonation (can imply that a questions is being asked) and stress, and the ways context can change a word's meaning. *(Continued on next page.)*

Based upon my own research and experience, this incorrect emphasis upon the Western/Greek over Hebraic is a direct result of anti-Semitism, which is synonymous with anti-Judaism. At times, this non-biblical concept is expressed in the statement: "We are New Testament Christians!" Perhaps, a better biblical way to state this is to say "We are followers of the Messiah and the Word of God."

From the time of Emperor Constantine until now, most Western theologians and Bible teachers interpret the Bible through a Greek, Roman-Greco or Western mindset.

Even though Thomas Aquinas knew that part of the New Testament was written in Hebrew, he allowed the prevailing culture of his day, along with the world view of the Catholic Church, to shape his thinking and writing.

Today, we know that much, if not all, of the New Testament was written in either Aramaic or Hebrew; not Greek. What may have been written in Greek was written through a Hebraic cultural lens.

The danger of Greek thinking is that an American can read the Bible cover to cover and the way he or she lives remains the same.

Syntax involves the best way to form a sentence to convey the correct meaning. For example, "Tracy sang all the way to church" is more descriptive than "the trip to church was full of singing."

Phonetics involves how a sound is made.

Semantics reveals the hidden meaning behind what is communicated. For example, to say "You have reached your destination" and "This is the last stop on your trip" may appear to mean the same thing, but when we look closer, there are subtle differences as to the meaning.

Yes, the person may agree with various Scriptures, and "believe" God is the Creator and Jesus the Savior, but it is merely a mental acknowledgement of the biblical facts. (Demons do this much. Reference Matthew 8:29 or Luke 4:34.)

If we are to understand the Bible, and what it means to be a follower of Jesus Christ, then we need to understand it hebraically; not through the lens of the Greek language or culture. This is not something to take lightly. It is profound!

We are so far removed from understanding God's Word, as it was understood when it was written and as it was understood in the time of the Early Church, it can cost a person their eternal life; even though the person "knows" the facts.

Let me give you a couple of examples: Matthew 5:17, "Do not think that I have come to *abolish the Law* or the Prophets; I have not come to abolish them but *to fulfill them*." (ESV, italics added)

In the first century, Jesus, as with us today, spoke in idioms. Jesus had been accused of incorrectly teaching the *Tanakh* (the Hebrew Bible or Old Testament). The expression, *abolish the Law* or *fulfill the Law,* were terms used by rabbis when they discussed the Bible. When one rabbi or sage (a wise person) felt his colleague had misinterpreted a passage of Scripture, he would say, "You are destroying the Law!" In addition, the Greek word *plerosai* does not mean "to fulfill," but "to fill."

Too often students of the Bible think that Jesus came to fulfill all of the prophecies and the Law of the Old Testament before He ascended to the right hand of the Father (Mark 16:19), which is not the case. There are prophecies about the Messiah that are yet to be fulfilled.[45] In Matthew 5:17, Jesus' preceding statement makes it clear that He did not come to abolish or destroy the Law (*Torah*).

The fundamental issue is that *plerosai* should not be translated "to fulfill" but "to fill" in that the Messiah came to "*fill* the *Torah* and ethnical pronouncements of the Prophets *full* with their *complete meaning*, so that everyone can know all that obedience entails." [46]

If you are one who believes in the doctrine that stipulates that believers today are "not under the Law," then you most likely are not overly concerned with living out the Word of God so that others can see Christ in the way you live. The litmus test is this:

- ❑ Do you have to *tell others* that you are a Christian?[47]
- ❑ Do others know that you are a Christian because *they see* the fruit of the Spirit in your daily life?[48]
- ❑ Do others *see the works of the flesh* in your life?[49]
- ❑ Do others *seek you out* to know the truth?[50]

---

45 In Isaiah 11:1-9 we see several prophecies about the Messiah. Many of them have been fulfilled in Yeshua. Yet, some have not been fulfilled. The wolves are not yet lying down with lambs. Nursing children are not playing at the cobra's hole and the earth is not full of the knowledge of the LORD.

46 *The Complete Jewish Bible*, xli

47 John 13:34-35 "A new commandment I give to you, that you love one another: just as I have loved you, you also are to love one another. By this all people will know that you are my disciples, if you have love for one another."(ESV)

48 Galatians 5:22-23, "fruit of the Spirit is love, joy, peace, longsuffering, gentleness, goodness, faith, Meekness, temperance: against such there is no law." (KJV)

49 Galatians 5:19-21, "the works of the flesh are manifest, which are these; Adultery, fornication, uncleanness, lasciviousness, Idolatry, witchcraft, hatred, variance, emulations, wrath, strife, seditions, heresies, envyings, murders, drunkenness, revellings, and such like: of the which I tell you before, as I have also told you in time past, that they which do such things shall not inherit the kingdom of God." (KJV)

When we fail to understand Matthew 5:17 from a Hebrew perspective, we reach a false interpretation of the Bible. Therefore, often Greek/Western thinking opens the door for us to believe that Jesus put an end to the need for us to obey the commands of the Old Testament, the Ten Commandments included. Why? We incorrectly read into Matthew 5:17 something the text does not actually say.

If one of the Alt-Right protesters in Charlottesville, Virginia in August, 2017 (that chanted "The Jews will not replace us") were to read the word "Jew" or "law" in the New Testament, do you think he would bother to spend the time uncovering the underlying meaning of the passage or would his worldview serve as the means for interpretation?

Sadly, in all innocence, false conclusions arise when we interpret the Bible through our own cultural lens; which may be based upon an anti-Semitic, anti-Jewish, and/or a Greek foundation.

Abraham Heschel writes, "The Greeks learned in order to comprehend." The "Hebrews learned in order to revere" [to worship God]. "The modern man learns in order to use" the Word to his own end.[51]

To the Hebrew, the desire for learning was to allow for the person to better worship God. We Westerners want to learn techniques that we can apply when a situation is out of our control. We want to

---

50 Acts 19:15 "the evil spirit answered them, 'Jesus I know, and Paul I know about, but who are you?'" (KJV)

51 Abraham J. Heschel, *Between God and Man: An interpretation of Judaism from the Writings of Abraham Heschel* (New York: Free Press, 1959), 54.

fix things. Let me find a recipe from the Bible. We want the biblical recipe for things in life that we want to change.

To the Hebrew, God is the center of all things. To the Westerner, self is in the center of all things. This is why in the Western world a Bible study is better attended than a prayer meeting.

Normally, a Greek-minded person does not want to worship God by living a godly life with his or her whole life. Why? The Greek-minded person may say, "I only need to give a part of me to God." He or she is content with spending one hour a week in a church service.

A Hebrew-minded person is continuously in a state of worship. Granted, there are Jewish people today that have adopted a Greek, or even a pagan, mindset and lifestyle.

Westerners value academic achievements, while a biblical Hebrew values obedience. 1 Corinthians 1:22 states this difference, "For *Jews demand signs* and *Greeks seek wisdom*" (ESV, italics added). This difference is summed in the following phrase: **Doing** (*signs*) verses **knowing** (*wisdom*).

The Hebrew is concerned with *doing* what the Word teaches, while the Greek is content with just *knowing* what the Word says: Behavior verses Knowledge. This is why we are so concerned with having the "right doctrine," yet we are hardly at all concerned with living a godly life. We agree that we should "love our neighbor," yet we'll make sure that what we give our "neighbor in need" are things that we no longer want.

To the Western, Greek-thinking Christian, he or she feels secure because *I know about God and Jesus. I believe the Bible.*

To the Hebrew mind, word and deed are inseparable. To say this another way, to have words without the deeds equals to a lie.

To the Hebrew mind to repent and to believe go hand in hand. We turn from our old way of living and obey the Word of God; this is not an option. (See *Appendix D* for the story about Zacchaeus.)

The Serpent in the Garden in Genesis 3:4 told Eve "you will not die," go ahead and eat. Today, the Enemy of God is saying the same thing: God does not really mean what He has stated in the Bible! You only need to "believe," you do not have to "do what it says." For that matter, you do not even need to read it.

Not understanding the Word of God rightly can lead to false conversions.

Salvation is much more than saying a few words.

> James 1:25
>
> "But whoever looks intently into the perfect law that gives freedom, and continues in it--*not forgetting what they have heard, but doing it*--they will be blessed in what they do." (NIV, italics added) [52]

Hebrew mindset is NOT the same as the Western mindset.

---

52 (NIV) - Scripture quotations taken from the THE HOLY BIBLE, NEW INTERNATIONAL VERSION®, NIV® Copyright © 1973, 1978, 1984, 2011 by Biblica, Inc. ® Used by permission. All rights reserved worldwide.

This creates a profound shift in how we view and obey the Bible.

CHAPTER FOUR

Biblical vs Western Thinking: A Deeper Look

> According to the Greeks, the gods were constantly changing, and were unconcerned with the mundane affairs of man. One reason is because life in their view was seen as linear. Time was an endless point in the past and continued to an endless point in the future.
>
> The God of scriptural thought is cyclical not linear. He brings to His creation cycles, cycles of righteousness and instruction. You can see this clearly in His creation.
>
> In Hebrew thought, YHWH never changes. He is immutable and is not like man. If He changed how could we trust Him.
>
> Man changes and is constantly evolving and progressing and in his fallen state thinks God must change with him.[53]

Based upon the teachings of the Bible, God knows the end from the beginning. In the Beginning what God established or planned has an eternal application. Basically, when God sets a future event in motion (future as it applies to us humans), in an eternal, divine sense;

53 The Way Biblical Fellowship teaching on May 11, 2016. http://thewaybiblicalfellowship.com/2016/05/11/the-hebrew-vs-the-greek-mindset-100516/ Accessed September 23, 2017.

the "future event" has already taken place. With this in mind, when did the sacrifice of the Messiah take place from God's perspective?[54]

As the Messiah was planned from the beginning of time, in God's perspective, it was a done deal long before the actual birth of Christ Jesus. Therefore, theologically speaking, when Abraham "believed the LORD" (Genesis 15:6) and this belief was "counted it to him as righteousness", Abraham's belief included the Scriptures about the Messiah even though the prophecies had not yet been written down[55] nor had the Word become flesh.[56] This also includes every believer from Abraham to Ruth, from the thief on the cross to Cornelius, as well as all believers since. (Note: If this paragraph just scrambled your theological brains that is okay. The passage below from Isaiah 55 may calm you down.)

> Isaiah 55:8-9
>
> For my thoughts are not your thoughts, neither are your ways my ways, declares the Lord. For as the heavens are higher than the earth, so are my ways higher than your ways and my thoughts than your thoughts. (ESV)

---

54 Revelation 13:8, "…the Lamb slain from the foundation of the world" (KJV). 1 Peter 1:20, "He was chosen before the creation of the world, but was revealed in these last times for your sake" (NIV).

The fall of mankind did not interfere with God's purpose in creating us. God is omniscient and there is nothing that occurs that He is unaware or surprised by. God does not run after Satan trying to clean up the mess he creates. The Sacrifice of the Messiah has already covered it.

55 Genesis 3:6, 15:6, Romans 4:3

56 John 1:1-5, 14

The most righteous and brilliant theologian of all time is no comparison to the Creator! Forgive me if I seem caustic. Look around you. Look up at the night sky. Ask a doctor about how the human body functions. There is more to God and His plans than He has chosen to tell us. You know, it is okay for us not to understand God's strategies fully; even when it comes to soteriology.[57]

Back to our topic at hand; *Biblical vs Western Thinking: A Deeper Look*. In Hebrew thought, God's nature is intimately connected to His commands. At times, we may confess that God is one and does not change, yet contradict this "confession" in our doctrinal statements or beliefs. At other times, our doctrinal statements are revised to stay in step with the shifting sands of culture change.

Believing things *about God* is not the same as *believing God.*

To God, there are no Old or New Testament. The separation of the Bible into two parts was done by the hand of man. There is only one covenant with humankind and it is found in the covenant God made with Abraham (and repeated to Isaac and Jacob). This covenant has two parts. This covenant involves Israel (Jacob) and the nations (the non-Jewish people). We'll revisit the Abrahamic Covenant later.

The biblical view of God as YHWH [yeh-ho-vaw'] is far greater than we Westerners grasp with our Greek-based thinking. Some theologians and pastors act as if they know how God views every situation in life. Some even think they can effectively expound with

57 Soteriology is the study of salvation.

complete accuracy each and every Scripture in the Bible. That is arrogance at its best.

We only know the part of God that He has chosen to reveal to us. God is infinite and it is completely beyond our capacity to understand Him in His fullness. Instead of trying to confine God to our limited human understanding and our best descriptive language, biblical thinking urges us to pursue a relationship with Him. It is through this relationship that greater understanding is possible, whereas the intellectual interplay of our reasoned-out ideas often results in the inflation of one another's ego at best and division among believers at worse.[58]

When it comes to worship of God, unlike the biblical model, the Greek mindset wants to worship in a definite manner and in a specific location. The biblical and Hebrew mindset is one that sees worship as a continuous act. There is no separation from what may be called secular or religious. There is no allowance for dualism.

Worship of God is a 24/7/365 event. Colossians 3:23-24 reflects this mindset. "Whatever you do, work heartily, as for the Lord and not for men, knowing that from the Lord you will receive the inheritance as your reward. You are serving the Lord Christ (ESV).

---

58 Proverbs 6:16-19 "There are six things that the LORD hates, seven that are an abomination to him: haughty eyes, a lying tongue, and hands that shed innocent blood, a heart that devises wicked plans, feet that make haste to run to evil, a false witness who breathes out lies, and one who sows discord among brothers." (ESV) It does not seem plausible for a person to be on God's Hate List and His Love List at the same time.

Based upon Colossians 3:23-24, when we go to work we are in (a biblical sense) worshipping Him as we do so. When I seek to meet my family's needs, I am worshipping God.

Why is this the biblical way? The text in Colossians we just read tells us that all we do, we do as unto the LORD. This also reflects the unity of a person's life. Greek thinking wants us to treat life as a pie with each slice being a different part of it. As such, we may only give God a slice or two of the whole pie, e.g., "I'll give God Wednesday evenings and Sunday mornings" or "I'll tithe 10% of my net income." The biblical mindset sees life as a whole. We give it all to God or we give Him nothing.

Biblically speaking, God, through His Word, has instructed us as to how to care for the earth, our physical bodies, our neighbors, the poor, our families, our money, our vocations, our relationship with Him, and times we are to rest.

An understanding of the Hebrew mindset is found in Ezekiel 36:27, "And I will put my spirit within you, and cause you to walk in my statutes, and ye shall keep my judgments, and do them" (KJV).

In the *Book of Second Opinions*, which is based on Western-Greek thinking, we want Ezekiel 36:27 to read "And I will put my spirit within you, and cause you to have peaceful thoughts about life and God when you attend church on Sunday."[59]

Do you see a difference in these two translations?

---

59 The Way Biblical Fellowship teaching on May 11, 2016. http://thewaybiblicalfellowship.com/2016/05/11/the-hebrew-vs-the-greek-mindset-100516/ Accessed September 23, 2017.

When it comes to salvation, Greek thought is having the right doctrine, even if you do not live by it. It means to believe the right things only. Often our doctrine is but one slice of the entire Bible, as if to imply the rest of God's Word is secondary to that which we have chosen for "our doctrine." Maybe that's why we have so many denominations; each has a separate slice of the theological pie. In actuality, to be saved means to be released from the evil things of this world. This includes that which divides believers.

Based upon Proverbs 6, "the Lord hates" anyone "who stirs up conflict in the community." (Proverbs 6:16-19; ESV) Separate denominations do not unite the corporate body of believers.

To have the right doctrine means to have the right and correct knowledge about God. Education and intellect are important to the Greek person. Things like "Pray the Sinner's Prayer to Be Saved" are based in Greek thought. In Greek thinking, salvation has a lot to do with what is "thought or spoken." Little concern is really placed on "doing" anything. (Do you see Descartes' influence?)

To the Hebrew mind salvation involves the body, soul and spirit. Salvation involves all areas of life. We do the right things as a direct result of trusting God for salvation. This is reflected in Matthew 5:13 about us being "the salt of the earth." As such, and because of our salvation, we are fully engaging all aspects of life as we obey God's Word. On purpose, we turn aside from all that is contrary or offensive to God and His Word: no hatred, no jealously, no greed, etc.

When it comes to prayer, the Greek thinking person only prays when there is a need. The Hebrew prays always for all things. Greeks pray with their eyes shut as they focus inwardly. The Hebrew prays with their eyes open as they look into the heavens. At times, Greeks pray for others to hear them praying. The Hebrew has many short prayers. His prayers are both ritual and spontaneous and full of "thank-you" to God. Ephesians 5:20 reflect the Hebrew perspective, "giving thanks always and for everything to God" (ESV).

Acts 3:1 tells us that "Peter and John went to the Temple one afternoon to take part in the three o'clock prayer service." The three o'clock prayer service was one of the three set times of prayer, both in Judaism and the Early Church, as validated by Peter and John. Grasp the teaching done by Peter and John! They modeled the historic Hebrew practice of prayer. Why don't we do it today? (Please do not say, "I am not under the Law!")

In 1 Thessalonians 5:16-18 we are challenged to "pray without ceasing". During the First century the established times of prayer were 9:00 am (the 3rd hour), noon (the 6th hour), and 3:00 pm (the 9th hour). It was understood that part of the command to "pray without ceasing" was to observe these three times of prayer. Obedience to this would afford corporate prayer at these set hours each and every day. Prayer offered in this manner diminishes "self" as the entire community focuses upon *Elohim*![60] Think about it. What if every believer in the whole earth all stopped and prayed at these three times each day?

---

60 For a complete study on the depth and meaning of *Elohim*, reference Dr. Michael S. Heiser's book, *The Unseen Realm* (Lexham Press, 2015).

The "*Shema* is a pledge of allegiance to the Lord God of Israel that excludes allegiance to any other gods."[61] We non-Jewish believers should adopt the *Shema* and likewise proclaim that God is the only One we are to worship! Observant Jews do this because it is a biblical commandment.

What about us non-Jewish believers? This same concept is taught by Jesus in Matthew 22:36-40.

> Matthew 22:36-40
>
> 36 "Teacher, which is the great commandment in the Law?" 37
> And he said to him, "You shall love the Lord your God with all
> your heart and with all your soul and with all your mind. 38
> This is the great and first commandment. 39 And a second is
> like it: You shall love your neighbor as yourself. 40 On these

---

61 Pronounced: shuh-MAH or SHMAH, Alternate Spellings: *Sh'ma, Shma.* The *Shema* refers to a couple of lines from the book of Deuteronomy (6:4-5), that became a daily prayer in Ancient Israelite tradition. The *Shema* gets its name from the first Hebrew word of the prayer in Deuteronomy 6:4, "Listen, Israel, the Lord is our God, the Lord alone." The English word "listen" renders the Hebrew word "s*hema.*" "Listen, Israel, the Lord is our God, the Lord alone, and you shall love the Lord your God with all your heart, all your being, and all your might." Deut. 6:4-5. In Ancient Hebrew, there is no present-tense verb equivalent to the English verb "is." There is a word for "was" (Heb. *hayah*) and "will be" (Heb. *yihyeh*), but "is" doesn't exist; rather, two words are put next to each other and the word "is" is inferred. The problem in translating and interpreting the *Shema* arises from the fact that it's made of two back-to-back sentences that lack the word "is." In Hebrew, the prayer consists of four nouns in a row. Hebrew: YHWH *'elohenu* YHWH *ekhad.* English: Lord our God Lord one. The *Shema* isn't trying to make a philosophical statement about God's essence or being (that God is "one"). Rather, the *Shema* is a pledge of allegiance to the Lord God of Israel that excludes allegiance to any other gods. (Source: Timothy Mackie, https://www.thebibleproject.com/blog/what-is-the-shema, accessed October 27, 2017.

> two commandments depend all the Law and the Prophets." (ESV)

As earlier stated, Descartes introduced Westerners to the non-biblical concept of dualism. Dualism is a concept that has its roots in Greek thinking. Basically, a human being exists in two parts: flesh and soul. The idea of dualism is that these two aspects of life are separated and the events of life fall into one category or the other; not both.

In dualism, one part is the flesh and therefore is mortal. The flesh contains our physical body, the physical world, and all that is considered carnal. On the other hand, we have the opposite to the flesh, which is the soul. The soul involves the mind, will and emotions; the things that are invisible and eternal. These are what Greek thinking deems to be holy or godly.

This dualism imposes upon the Western world a non-biblical concept about life that creates division within each person and within our community. Dualism states that the soul of a person is what goes to heaven. Dualism teaches that knowledge and correct thinking feed the soul. Morals and ethics are intellectual concepts, therefore, according to the Greek mindset, are for the soul.

With dualism as the backdrop, to the Greek thinking person, the heart (the soul) is good and the body (the flesh) is evil. Since only the soul will enter heaven, it is not important what the body does or does not do.

Dualism gives birth to the concept that a person can be "spiritual" and, at the same time, NOT obey the teachings of the Bible.

This separation, this dualism, does not occur in the biblical or Hebrew mindset. This is why Greek thinking Christians strive for more and more knowledge to feed the soul. Yet, at times, to varying degrees, fail in living the Word of God.

Look around you at the people you go to church with. How many are REALLY concerned about reaching people with the Gospel message? Dualism is poisonous to the Church.

Dualism is a lie from the Enemy and is expressed through the work of Anti-Messiah. Why? This concept is contrary to the Word of God! Psalm 128:1 (ESV), "Blessed is everyone who fears the LORD, who walks in his ways!" James 1:22, speaks about us being "doers of the word, and not hearers only, deceiving yourselves." To be "doers of the word", and walk in the "ways" of God, means that we live each day according to the teachings of the Bible. Both the flesh and the soul are obedient to the Word.

> Acts 26:20
>
> but declared first to those in Damascus, then in Jerusalem and throughout all the region of Judea, and also to the Gentiles, that they should *repent* and *turn to God*, ***performing deeds in keeping with their repentance.*** (ESV, bold and italics added)

Luke relays Paul's message that believers "should turn from their sins to God and then do deeds consistent with that repentance."[62]

Without works or deeds, there is an absence of validation for the believer's profession of faith.

The Greek mindset is content with just knowing what the Bible says with little regard to living the ways of God. To live a life conformed to the Greek mindset may result in the ultimate deception and cost you an eternal life with God.

> 2 John 1:6
> "And this is love, that we walk according to his commandments; this is the commandment, just as you have heard from the beginning, ***so that you should walk in it.***" (ESV, bold and italics added)

To know the commands of the Bible and not live according to them is self-deception at its best.

> Mark 11:12-14
> 12 On the following day, when they came from Bethany, he was hungry. 13 And *seeing in the distance a fig tree in leaf, he went to see if he could find anything on it.* When he came to it, he found nothing but leaves, for it was not the season for figs. 14 And he

62 Acts 26:20, CBJ

> said to it, "May no one ever eat fruit from you again." And his disciples heard it. (ESV, italics added)

This fig tree, if it had visible leaves, should have had unripe fruit since the unripe fruit was visible before the spring leaves![63] The point is this: God expects us to have fruit of righteous living that is visible in our entire being (body and soul). If not, the fate of this tree is our fate.

If we live our lives functioning as Greek-thinking individuals, even if we are unaware of the differences, and then add the ingredient known as anti-Judaism (anti-Semitism) to the recipe, the result is a formula for theological persuasion that creates the environment found in many of our Western local churches. This is why so many Western Christians feel that the *Tanakh* (the Old Testament) is a collection of myths, legends, and stories designed only to teach metaphorical lessons or serve as typology for us today.

Our Greek-thinking is part of the reason that only a slight majority of Christians (55%) strongly agree that the Bible is accurate in all of the principles it teaches; about half (47%) of the Christians believe that Satan is merely a symbol of evil; 49% say that the Holy Spirit is only a symbol but not a living entity; about one-third (33%) of the self-defined Christians agree that the Bible, Koran and Book of Mormon all teach the same truths.[64]

> When asked if they had previously "heard of the Great Commission," half of U.S. churchgoers (51%)

63 David H. Stern, *Jewish New Testament Commentary* (Jewish New Testament Publications, Inc.: Clarksville, MD, 1992,1996), 96

64 Source: *The Barna Group*

> say they do not know this term. It would be reassuring to assume that the other half who know the term are also actually familiar with the passage known by this name, but that proportion is low (17%). Meanwhile, "the Great Commission" does ring a bell for one in four (25%), though they can't remember what it is. Six percent of churchgoers are simply not sure whether they have heard this term "the Great Commission" before.[65]

Left alone, Greek thinking Christians overly focus on the grace of God, therefore the concept of being a doer of the Word is not relevant for today. We propagate that all a person has to do is speak the words found in a "Sinner's Prayer" and he or she has a ticket to spend eternity with Jesus. If there is no outward evidence that Christ is the center of your life (beyond attending a Sunday church service) and any evidence of spiritual regeneration is only based simply upon what you have said, then you have possibility believed a lie.

When it comes to the Bible, it always involves interpretation AND application of what is written.

A good Western Christian is, at times, only a "knower" of the Word. This is a dangerous place to be!

65 www.barna.com/research/half-churchgoers-not-heard-great-commission, accessed April 4, 2018.

James 2:17-18

So also *faith by itself, if it does not have works, is dead.* But someone will say, "You have faith and I have works." Show me your faith apart from your works, and *I will show you my faith by my works.* (ESV, italics added)

To me, as a biblical thinking Christian, what I believe determines what I do.

John 1:14

And the Word became flesh and dwelt among us, and we have seen his glory, glory as of the only Son from the Father, full of grace and truth. (ESV)

To have a biblical mindset is to never stop growing in the Word *and* doing that which has been learned. Never forget that it was the Word of God that became flesh (John 1:14). When we grow in our application of the Word learned we grow in our relationship with the Messiah.

As my relationship with God the Father, and with His Son (my Savior and Friend) grows, and as I give more of my life to the filling and leading of the Holy Spirit, each day is a new beginning in this journey we call life. I am here to serve God and I must continually adjust to His leading and not follow my own desires.

To the biblical thinking person, love is not an emotional concept. Love for God is expressed in our choices and preferences.

This is expressed in John 14:15 (ESV), "If ye love me, ye will keep my commandments." But one may say that "I am no longer under the law." This is correct, if you are referring to the "law" as being the enslavement to sin. If a person loves the Lord Jesus, then the person must obey His commandments; the imperatives of the Bible. It is a natural by-product of a Christ-centered life.

Proverbs 3:1-4 tells us to not forget the law; the teachings of the Bible. It says that peace will be added to our lives when we obey the teachings of the Bible.

In the Greek way of thinking, emotion is central to enjoying life and greatly influences the decisions we make. Therefore, the "emotion" needs to be sustained or the commitment associated with the initial emotion stops. This is why so many Christian marriages end in divorce; the emotional attraction is gone.

In biblical (Hebrew) thought, emotion is a byproduct of a previous commitment. The commitment is the driving force; not one's emotions. Because many Christians in the United States operate under a Greek-based mindset, when the emotion is no longer satisfactory, they stop following the Lord and the teachings of the Bible. For example, the last time you did not have your "prayer time with the LORD," was it because you did not "feel" like doing it? Due to the level of emotion generated through certain songs, even our times of worship may become an emotional end-in-itself.

Loving God and loving our neighbor are one in the same in biblical thought. To do one without the other is a lie. Both parts united equal truth. I've heard it can be said that "we are the sum parts of our lives - the sum total of all of our relationships."[66]

Loving God and loving our neighbor extends beyond our relationship with God. This includes our relationships with every person that crosses our path. If I love God, then I will love each person regardless of their social or economic standing, or even their ethnicity.

In biblical thought you are defined by what you do. (Recall Matthew 7:21?[67]) If you say, "I am a chess player," but never play chess then you are not really a chess player. Likewise, if you say you are a Christian and do not follow the teachings of the Bible then you are not a Christian. This is why the organized local churches in the USA have failed to be salt and light to our society at large (Matthew 5:13-16). We "talk" about being Christians, but we often "live" like pagans. God is not at the center of our world; self is!

Remember John 14:15, "If you love me, you will keep my commandments" (ESV), and 1 John 2:6 "whoever says he abides in him ought to walk in the same way in which he walked" (ESV).

When it comes to worship, a Western-Greek mindset is satisfied with going to the "place" of worship. In contrast, to the biblical/Hebrew mind, worship is an ongoing lifestyle.

---

66 Source unknown

67 Matthew 7:21 "Not everyone who says to me, 'Lord, Lord,' will enter the kingdom of heaven, but the one who does the will of my Father who is in heaven." (ESV)

> Greek thought views the world through the mind (abstract thought). Ancient Hebrew thought views the world through the senses (concrete thought) [68]
>
> Concrete thought is the expression of concrete concepts and ideas in ways that can be seen, touched, smelled, tasted and/or heard. All five of the senses are used when speaking and hearing and writing and reading in the Hebrew language. An example of this can be found in Psalm 1:3; "he is like a tree planted by streams of water, which yields its fruit in season, and whose leaf does not wither". In this passage we have concrete words expressing abstract thoughts, such as a tree (one who is upright, righteous), streams of water (grace), fruit (good character) and an un-withered leaf is (prosperity). [69]
>
> Abstract thought is the expression of concepts and ideas in ways that cannot be seen, touched, smelled, tasted or heard. Hebrew never uses abstract thought as English does. Examples of abstract thought can be found in Psalms 103:8; "the LORD is compassionate and gracious, slow to anger, abounding in love". As you noticed I said that Hebrew uses concrete and not abstract thoughts, but here we have such abstract concepts as compassionate, gracious, anger, and love in a Hebrew passage. Actually these are abstract English words translating the original Hebrew concrete words. The translators often translate this way because the original Hebrew makes no sense when literally translated into English.[70]

Earlier I mentioned the meaning of anger and what it meant in Hebrew. For the sake of clarity, I'll restate what I have said earlier.

---

68 The Way Biblical Fellowship teaching on May 11, 2016. http://thewaybiblicalfellowship.com/2016/05/11/the-hebrew-vs-the-greek-mindset-100516/ Accessed September 23, 2017.

69 Ibid.

70 Ibid.

The Hebrew word translated into the English word "anger" literally means "nose." When someone is very angry, and as his breathing increases, their "nostrils begin to flare." Therefore, a Hebrew sees anger as "the flaring of the nose (nostrils)." If the English translator had literally translated the Hebrew words "slow to nose," it just wouldn't make any sense to us. [71] As you can see, at times we lose the beauty of the meaning of the text when it is translated into English, especially when the translators did not understand the culture and the idioms. At times, even more is lost when that which is translated is taught using only a Greek mindset.

One more aspect to understanding a biblical mindset verses a Greek one is what is meant by the English word "lie." Usually we define a lie as not telling the truth. In ancient Hebrew, a lie was "disagreeing with God's truth or not fulfilling your purpose or function in life."[72]

If I know God's Word and I do not agree with it or live His Word, then I am a liar.

Not fulfilling God's purpose for your life makes you out to be a liar. This is further expressed in that we are to be the "salt of the earth" in Matthew 5:13. Also, we see this concept in Matthew 5:16, "…let your light shine before others, so that they may see your good works and give glory to your Father who is in heaven" (ESV). It seems that we

---

71 http://ancient-hebrew.org/m/articles_thought.html accessed September 23, 2017.

72 Ibid.

American Christians want others to only "hear" what we say. Please do not "look at the way" I live!

Consider these two Scriptures:

Ecclesiastes 12:13

The end of the matter; all has been heard. Fear God *and* keep his commandments, for this is the whole duty of man. (ESV, italics added)

1 John 2:4

Whoever says "I know him" *but does not keep his commandments* is a liar, and the truth is not in him (ESV, italics added)

If I know God's Word, I will do what God's Word says.

As I finish up our covering of the *Biblical vs Western Thinking,* let me summarize by saying that I hope you no longer believe that all you have to *do* is think the right things, *say* the right things, or *agree* with the right doctrine in order to be saved. If you really know the Word and you really know the Messiah, then your life, your thoughts, your attitudes, and everything else about you will be changed.

Romans 12:12

I appeal to you therefore, brothers, by the mercies of God, to present your bodies as a living sacrifice, holy and acceptable to

God, which is your spiritual worship. Do not be conformed to this world, but be transformed by the renewal of your mind, that by testing you may discern what is the will of God, what is good and acceptable and perfect. (ESV)

Philippians 2:5
Let this mind be in you, which was also in Christ Jesus: (KJV)

We are saved by grace if your faith produces a changed life.

CHAPTER FIVE

Deception #1

The Authority of the Institutional Church has usurped the authority of God

> Some of the worst havoc wrought to the Christian faith has been a direct result of unscriptural forms of church structure…Under Christ's name an elaborately structured institution emerged that corrupted the simple, family structure of the apostolic churches, robbed God's people of their lofty position and ministry in Christ, and exchanged Christ's supremacy over His people for supremacy of the instructional church.[73]

As we unfold the *First Deception of the End Times*, let me say that this study is the direct result of observing the condition of individual believers and local churches during the past 40 years of ministry. Some may say that I only interacted with carnal-Christians. I wish that was the case. I have personally taught and mentored over two hundred pastors and elders that crossed many denominations in five

73 Alexander Strauch, *Biblical Eldership* (Littleton, CO: Lewis and Roth Publishers, 1995), 101.

countries. This is in addition to an unknown number of people that the *institution of the church* calls "the laity."[74]

What I often noticed was that the believers and church leaders were good people. If asked, they would tell me that Jesus was the Lord of their lives. Yet, if I asked how they were engaged in Great Commission work – *were they in fact currently engaged in making disciples* – they would often stare back with blank eyes.

Over 90% of the Christians I have known have not introduced one person to the Father, Son and Holy Spirit. *They are surfers that never went near the water.*

Much of my current research is driven by my desire to understand the reasons for the current lethargic state-of-affairs in Western Christendom. There are only a handful of local churches that reflect the character traits recorded in the Book of Acts (Reference your answers in Chapter Two).

My hope is that if the source of the "sickness" (this lethargic behavior) can be discovered, then a cure may be found. Yes, we can say that "Jesus is the answer." However, the individuals I have interacted with know all about Jesus as the Savior (emphasis on *knowing* - mental

74 If you go to www.merriam-webster.com, the definition given for laity is 'the people of a religious faith as distinguished from its clergy" (accessed April 4, 2018). This is the realty that most churchgoers live by! Yet, this definition, although widely accepted, is NOT biblical. This non-biblical distinction between vocational or professional ministers and all the other believers (the laity) started when the role of the institutional church replaced or usurped the authority of the local church in the selection of leaders (what we call ordination). A local church should have elders and/or deacons, however, these individuals are not above the other members. We are all part of the priesthood (1 Peter 2:9).

acknowledgment). Most have even made a profession of faith, been baptized in water, and own one or more Bibles. Yet, something is missing; a life of obedience to the Bible.

> "The truth is, if you take a student who has no position on the millennium and send him [or her] to Westminster Seminary, he [or she] will probably come out amillennialist.[75] If you take the same student and send him [or her] to Dallas Seminary, [the student] is even more likely to come out a premillennialist. [76] There will be few exceptions to this rule. Our environment, our theological traditions, and our teachers have much more to do with what we believe than we realize … I have observed that the majority of what Christians believe is not derived from their own patient and careful study of the Scriptures." [77]

Lastly, too many people align themselves with one Western theological perspective or another; one denomination or another. Yet, their knowing about Jesus and the Bible has not changed the way they live and interact with one another. On many levels they act just like the people in the pagan society in which they live. If the Word of God, the whole Bible, is not the standard by which we are to live by, then society will set the standard for us. For many churchgoers this is the case.

Let's have a brief history lesson. First, let's look at Pope Boniface VIII (AD 1294-1303). In the year 1302, a little over 700 years ago, Pope Boniface decreed that "we are obliged to believe and

---

75 Amillennialist basically reject the belief that Jesus will have a literal, thousand-year-long, physical reign on the earth.

76 Premillennialist believe that Jesus will return and reign for one-thousand years.

77 Jack Deere, *Surprised by the Power of the Spirit,* (Zondervan: Grand Rapids, MI, 1993), 47.

maintain that the Church is one, holy, catholic, and also apostolic. We believe in her firmly and we confer with simplicity that outside of her [the Church] there is neither salvation nor the remission of sin”. [78]

What did Pope Boniface VIII say?

Boniface said that if a person was not part of the Roman Catholic Church, the person could not experience salvation.

Basically, this Pope moved the authority of the Gospel message from the Messiah, the work of Holy Spirit and us the witnesses of the Gospel message; to the entity, *the institution* we call the Church. Not the corporate body of believers, but, in his view, the leadership and institution known as the Roman Catholic Church.

This mindset is very much alive today and is reflected in our institutions made with the brick and mortar and defined by doctrines, dogma, and endless traditions. Today we call these institutions churches. We speak of these institutions with much love, “My church…”

This is expressed by our viewing the “church” through our institutional lens. This perspective is revealed when we say that we “are *going* to church.”

> Romans 16:5a
>
> Greet also the *church in their house.* Greet my... (ESV, italics added)

---

78 Carroll, *Constantine's Sword*, 315

> Philemon 1:1-2
>
> Paul, a prisoner for Christ Jesus, and Timothy our brother, To Philemon our beloved fellow worker and Apphia our sister and Archippus our fellow soldier, and *the church in your house*: (ESV, italics added)

This is more than semantics (a play on words). We have the biblical model of the true Church. We also have the counterfeit, the man-made, brick-n-mortar model of the church.

We greatly devalue the individual believer when we filter everything through the corporate entity we now call the church.

Matthew 9:37 states that Jesus told His disciples that "…'The harvest is plentiful, but the workers are few.'" Did Jesus mean to communicate to us that we the workers are to go and get people to come to the church building? No! Yet, that is what many Christians do week after week. We invite people to come to "our church" so they can meet Jesus through the message from "our pastor."

Often, to a person that is enslaved to the Kingdom of Darkness, they will never step foot in a church building. Yet, the popular church-growth model is to attempt to do this very thing. It is like we lost sight of the "go" part of the Great Commission and inserted the word "come."[79]

Based upon the Pope's decree that the Church is the avenue for people to meet Jesus, there is no longer a need to pray for the workers to go into the harvest fields. The harvest just needs to come to the barn (aka, church building) to be saved. All of us have been a part of the common practice of "inviting someone to church so they can be saved." I am not being facetious; this is a critical issue that has all but killed the Western Christian Church.[80]

Allow the implications of this ruling by the Pope settle into how we define and view the local church today.

The Pope's decree, over 700 years later, is still in effect today. Active churchgoers, for the most part, are unable to go and make disciples outside of the paradigm of the local church institution! This is a very dangerous place for us to be.

A friend told me recently that "his church was teaching their older members how to witness." He was so excited that I could not bring myself to tell him that, if you have to teach them *how to be a witness*, the chances were pretty good that *they have not witnessed anything to testify about.*

---

79 Matthew 28:16-20. Now the eleven disciples went to Galilee, to the mountain to which Jesus had directed them. 17 When they saw him, they worshiped him; but some doubted. 18 And Jesus came and said to them, "All authority in heaven and on earth has been given to me. 19 **Go therefore and make disciples** of all nations, baptizing them in the name of the Father and of the Son and of the Holy Spirit, 20 and teaching them to obey everything that I have commanded you. And remember, I am with you always, to the end of the age." (NRSV)

80 The average local church spends about 22% on the building and only 5% on foreign and domestic missions. Source: *How Churches Spend their Money*, http://www.pnwumc.org, accessed March 1, 2018.

In 1990, Greg Ogden wrote a book titled, *The New Reformation.* On page 29, he states:

> We are in the midst of something as radical as a paradigm shift from the church as institution to the church as an organism...the church in its essence is nothing less than a life - pulsating people who are animated by the indwelling presence of Jesus Christ. [81]

How I wish Greg's statement was more widespread. What I have personally seen is an increase in the number of Christians exit the brick and mortar institutions.

Why are they leaving? As we get closer to the End Time, the fog is lifting. The façade is being discovered. These people love the Lord, but they are tired of the institution and the traditions of men. Yet, they have not been equipped to live the Christian life outside of the local church model.

The really sad thing is the people that are active in the brick and mortar buildings are often clueless about what has taken place. Often, those in the brick and mortar buildings, unknowingly, want the Pope's decrees to be obeyed! They want people to come to their church!

The Pope declared "that outside of her [the Church institution] there is neither salvation nor the remission of sin." [82] The indoctrination, the deception, is so effective, so complete, that they have eyes but cannot see.

---

81 Greg Ogden, *The New Reformation* (Zondervan Publishing House: Grand Rapids, MI, 1990), 29

82 Carroll, *Constantine's Sword*, 315

John 12:40

"He has blinded their eyes and hardened their heart, lest they see with their eyes, and understand with their heart, and turn, and I would heal them." (ESV)

2 Corinthians 4:4

In their case the god of this world has blinded the minds of the unbelievers, to keep them from seeing the light of the gospel of the glory of Christ, who is the image of God. (ESV)

Isaiah 6:10

"Make the heart of this people dull, and their ears heavy, and blind their eyes; lest they see with their eyes, and hear with their ears, and understand with their hearts, and turn and be healed." (ESV)

Matthew 15:14

"Let them alone; they are blind guides. And if the blind lead the blind, both will fall into a pit."

The point with spiritual blindness, regardless of the specific reason for the blindness, is that the Truth is hidden because the person that is blinded was not diligent in seeking the LORD or repentant of their sins, therefore, the Enemy took advantage of the opportunity.

I am NOT saying that the local church building is sinful.

I am NOT saying we should stop attending a local church that meets in a building.

I AM saying that the people that need to know the Messiah are in the fields that are ripe for harvest; from the communities around us to the ends of the earth. We MUST GO to them!

The love affair that some Christians have with the local church building is an Achilles heel in our reaching the lost. When the last days of Jacob's Trouble[83] occur, this model will prove disastrous. The Church outside of the Western world has a distinct advantage over us; therefore, we should learn from them.

The next point in our history lesson is Thomas Aquinas who lived from AD 1225 to 1274. Along with other theologians in the Catholic Church of his time period, when it came to the study of the Bible, Thomas Aquinas propagated the concept of "systematic intellectual" and "philosophical theology". [84]

Aquinas taught that "reason and debate" were sufficient to bring about salvation. (Do you see the Greek thinking?) *His focus was understanding with the mind as a means to salvation.* The role of the Holy Spirit is no longer required.[85] Basically, this idea supports the concept that "I can convince" an unbeliever to accept Christ solely through intellectual discourse. This concept is used when we take a person

---

83 See *Appendix F*

84 Carroll, *Constantine's Sword*, 301

85 Our spirit is drawn by the Holy Spirit to God. It is in our spirit where we initially commune with God. The Holy Spirit draws us to Christ through our spirit.
John 6:44, "No one can come to me unless the Father who sent me draws him. And I will raise him up on the last day." (ESV)
John 6:65, And he said, "This is why I told you that no one can come to me unless it is granted him by the Father." (ESV)

through "The Romans Road."[86] In that if "I" can draw a clear picture of hell, the non-believer will logically and rationally decide to "accept Jesus" based on said reasoning.

Thomas Aquinas' teaching puts forth the idea that by enough debate and by quoting enough Scriptures we can bring about salvation of the lost soul. Blend this concept with what the Pope did by elevating the role of the Church as an institution; it is a recipe for disaster. This model plays into the core of Greek thinking with self at the center of our lives. In the end, this elevates "self" to a place only God should have, especially in our efforts to reach the lost.

(AD 1302) Pope Boniface VIII decreed that "we are obliged to believe and maintain that the Church is one" and "outside of her [the Catholic Church] there is neither salvation nor the remission of sin". [87]

Trusting in our ability to convince a lost soul to accept Christ places a human being at the center of the call to salvation.

Recently I heard a pastor state his goals: I want to get the person "saved," then have him "baptized," and then have him "discipled into the services here at the church." This is what many of our institutional churches do. Unfortunately, this strategy does not agree with the Great Commission as presented in the Bible.

---

86 The Romans Road to salvation is a way of explaining the good news of salvation using verses from the Book of Romans. Using these verses is a method of explaining why a person needs salvation, how God provided salvation, how the person can receive salvation, and what are the results of salvation. This is all fine, except, little regard is given to the reality of John 6:44, John 6:65, et al, in that, before you complete the exchange with having the person say "A Sinner's Prayer," confirm that the person is in fact, at this moment, being drawn by the Holy Spirit to God. Why? If the Holy Spirit is NOT involved, then you have NOT led the person to Christ! But, the person believes salvation has occurred.

87 Carroll, *Constantine's Sword*, 315

John 6:44

No *one can come to me unless the Father who sent me draws him*. And I will raise him up on the last day. (ESV, italics added)

John 1:12-13

But to all who did receive him, who believed in his name, he gave the right to become children of God, who were born, *not of blood nor of the will of the flesh nor of the will of man, but of God.* (ESV, italics added)

2 Thessalonians 2:13-14

But we ought always to give thanks to God for you, brothers beloved by the Lord, because *God chose you as the first fruits to be saved*, through sanctification by the Spirit *and* belief in the truth. (ESV, italics added)

The work of the Holy Spirit precedes the testimony of our being a witness.

As noted in John 20:22, It is Christ that "...breathed on" the first followers. It was Christ who "said to them, 'Receive the Holy Spirit.'" Granted, each true Christian has the responsibility to be a witness to the lost; those without Christ. Even though we are used by God, it is the Holy Spirit that directs our steps (Galatians 5:25).

Based upon this shift in thinking, Thomas Aquinas made it official that man, not the Holy Spirit or even the Messiah, is now the deciding factor; the pivot point.

True or False: Human reasoning and salesmanship can win the lost person to Christ. Sadly, the institution of the Church is full of people that have been "persuaded" to accept Christ.

Did you know that "80%" of active churchgoers actually believe that it is their job to share the Gospel message? This is great, but, "61%" of [the 80%] have NOT shared their faith "in the previous six months".[88] Therefore, only two out of ten active church goers actually shares their faith on a regular basis.

From my own experiences, approximately nine out of ten churchgoers have never discipled another person (from being lost, to accepting Christ as Lord, to becoming a mature follower of God).

This is what Thomas Aquinas and the Catholic Church has done for us. Even today, we Protestants continue to be faithful to their legacy. We are programed to do ministry through the institution we call a church that is located in a building.

Sharing your faith should not be boiled down to you telling another person "where you attended church services on Sunday!"

It is one thing to share your faith, but are we able to make a disciple of the person? This goes far beyond sharing your testimony.

The rationale developed by Thomas Aquinas has become firmly established in our Protestant Churches. Where is the Holy Spirit in all of this?

---

88 The study conducted by LifeWay Research, http://www.lifeway.com/Article/research-survey-sharing-christ-2012, accessed September 5, 2017

Thomas Aquinas "articulated a philosophical rationale for the hierarchical order that the medieval Church embraced."[89] He also wrote "that it is absolutely necessary for salvation that every human creature be subject to the Roman Pontiff." [90] That is to say that he supported the authority of the institutional Church and the Pope for salvation. This gave birth to written creeds as a document apart from the whole written Word of God found in the Bible. We basically took a slice of the Bible and declared through our doctrine that this "slice" is more important than all of the rest of the Bible. (Do you see the Greek-based rationale at work here?)

Now we know what happened to the biblical model of elder-led local churches and part of the reason we have so many denominations.

We Protestants faithfully followed the Catholic Church's model, which followed the model of the Roman government. We do not call the leader of the congregation Priest, but Pastor. When it is all said and done, the framework of the Protestant Church (from our special chairs, candles, brass offering plates, sacred pieces of furniture, windows, traditions, etc.) imitates the Roman Catholic Church.

During the Reformation the Protestant's protested against the authoritative rule of the Catholic Church and its leadership structures. Protestants adopted a democratic form of church government, which was the most obvious change. Neither form of government was based upon the biblical model.

The primary issues that brought about the Reformation were a desire to get the focus back on the Bible, away from the influence of

89 Carroll, *Constantine's Sword*, 305
90 Ibid, 316

powerful church leaders, and a freedom from being dictated to by church tradition. The Reformation did NOT accomplish its goal. Take a look around at our local Protestant churches. Maybe it is time for yet another Reformation.

The Catholic Church did not change their view of the role and authority of the Church in regards to a person's salvation until 1953.[91] This official doctrine had been in place for over 600 years and would not change overnight. Keep in mind that the entire Western world had been under the teachings of the Catholic Church until the Reformation in the 16th century.

The break created by the Reformers from the Catholic Church was a convoluted rupture that took an enormous toll upon all of Christendom of the Western European countries. This period was a stain on the witness of the Christian Church during that period of time. It is not something that we need to celebrate; rather, we should collectively repent for the sins that led up to it.

Although the causes were many, due to the Reformation movement, religious tensions between Catholics and Protestants ran deep. The Thirty Years' War was one of the longest and most destructive conflicts.[92] The most conservative numbers put the death toll between 3 and 4 million.[93] The war was more or less between Catholics and Protestants and was fought between 1618 and 1648.

This was a war between professing Christians!

---

91 Ibid

92 Peter H. Wilson, *Europe's Tragedy: A New History of the Thirty Years War* (London: Penguin, 2010), 787

93 Geoffrey Parker, *The Thirty Years War* (New York: Routledge, 1984, 1997) p.188

Every Western local church has to some degree been influenced with the doctrines, and yes, the sins of the historic Church!

> The Protestant Reformation was the 16th-century religious, political, intellectual and cultural upheaval that splintered Catholic Europe, setting in place the structures and beliefs that would define the continent in the modern era. In northern and central Europe, reformers like Martin Luther, John Calvin and Henry VIII challenged (the Pope's) authority and questioned the Catholic Church's ability to define Christian practice. They argued for a religious and political redistribution of power … King Henry VIII (1491-1547) ruled England for 36 years, presiding over sweeping changes that brought his nation into the Protestant Reformation. He famously married a series of six wives in his search for political alliance, marital bliss and a healthy male heir. His desire to annul his first marriage without the Pope's approval led to the creation of a separate Church of England. Of his marriages, two ended in annulment, two in natural deaths and two (were beheaded) … for adultery and treason. [94]

> [As with Emperor] Constantine at the opening of the Council of Nicaea, [King] James delivered the opening address. [In doing so] He immediately set the tone and gave clear cues of what to expect. The doctrine and polity of the state Church of England was not up for evaluation and reconsideration [in the translation of the King James Bible].[95]

---

94 http://www.history.com/topics/reformation, accessed August 25, 2017

95 http://www.christianity.com/church/church-history/timeline/1601-1700/story-behind-king-james-bible-11630052.html, accessed August 25, 2017

Emperor Constantine (AD 272 to 337) looked at himself as the "vice-regent of God."[96] The way he saw things: God was in heaven, so he, as the Emperor, was here on earth to handle things for Him.

As the influence of Constantine grew, the authority structure within the emerging Church was shaped, not after the Bible, but the Roman government's model. The role of biblical elders and deacons was all but lost.

As the influence of the Pope, Thomas Aquinas, and the Emperor Constantine grew over the years, this in turn, redefined what was meant by the word "church." Many people in the Western world have only one understanding of the word church; that it is a building.

The English word "church" comes from a German word for "building" (*kirche*). In the Bible the word church comes from the word *ekklesia* (ek-klay-see'-ah) which means an assembly of people or people called-out by God.

Biblically speaking, the meaning of church is not a building or even a geographical location, but people.

Paul was not a "church planter" like preachers today that go by that name. Modern church planters, at times, are engaged in pulling people from one local church to the "new church" they are starting. Paul was a kingdom builder! Paul was teaching the whole Bible. He was gathering the new believers into small communities of believers.

---

96 W. H. C. Frend, *The Rise of Christianity* (Fortress Press: Philadelphia, PA ,1984), 523

Romans 16:5 says "… greet the church that is in their house." Paul refers to the believers in the house as the church. The New Testament local churches do not resemble what we know today as a church.

During the third and fourth centuries, what was considered "correct thinking" was defined by Emperor Constantine and NOT the Bible. Right thinking was further defined by the historic Catholic Church. Having a "choice" in matters affecting Christians and the meaning of the Bible was now defined for us by the official Church, the Emperor, and the Pope. The word choice became heresy in that if someone disagreed with the established opinion of "the Church," then, by default, they were labeled "heretics."

When Emperor Constantine I (a pagan sun-worshipper) came to power in AD 313, he legalized Christianity and on March 7, A.D. 321, his rule stated: "On the highly" respected "Day of the Sun let the magistrates and people residing in cities rest, and let all workshops be closed."[97]

This declaration by Constantine was not fully followed until the Council of Laodicea made its declaration about Sunday some forty odd years later.

The Sunday law was officially confirmed by the Pope. The Council of Laodicea in A.D. 364 decreed, "Christians shall not Judaize and be idle on Saturday but shall work on that day [Saturday]; but the Lord's Day [Sunday] they shall especially honour, and, as being

[97] *Codex Justinianus 3*.12.3, trans. Philip Schaff, *History of the Christian Church*, 5th ed. (New York, 1902), 3:380, note 1.

Christians, shall, if possible, do no work on that day. If, however, they are found Judaizing, they shall be shut out from Christ"[98]

Basically, if you observed the biblical Sabbath (Saturday), the official Church said that you had lost your salvation.

Notice the anti-Semitic charge to the people not to "Judaize and be idle on Saturday." In essence, the Church told the people to no longer pay attention to the foundation of our faith, which is found in the Old Testament.

> Isaiah 56:2-8
>
> "And the foreigners who join themselves to the LORD, to minister to him, to love the name of the LORD, and to be his servants, **everyone who keeps the Sabbath** and does not profane it, and holds fast my covenant—these I will bring to my holy mountain, and make them joyful in my house of prayer; their burnt offerings and their sacrifices will be accepted on my altar; for my house shall be called a house of prayer for all peoples." The Lord GOD, who gathers the outcasts of Israel, declares, "I will gather yet others to him besides those already gathered." (ESV, bold added)

As the Western Church devalued Israel (the Jewish people), and propagated the idea that "Israel had rejected the Messiah." The message that was carried forward to this very day is that God's Words recorded in the *Tanakh* (the Old Testament) are no longer important!

---

98 Charles J. Hefele, *A History of the Councils of the Church*, 2, (Edinburgh, 1876) 316.

The foundation upon which the New Testament, indeed the very salvation of "the nations",[99] was undermined. This opened the door to a very dangerous place for the Western Church. We, the non-Jewish believers were, by devaluing God's chosen people, Israel, elevated ourselves as God's chosen people. Man did this; NOT God. We have opened the door for God's wrath spoken in Genesis 12:3, "I will bless those who bless you [Israel] and him who dishonors you I will curse..." Consider the following Scriptures.

> Isaiah 42:6-7
>
> "I am the LORD; I have called you [Israel] in righteousness; I will take you [Israel] by the hand and keep you; I will give you [Israel] as a covenant for the people, **a light for the nations**, to open the eyes that are blind, to bring out the prisoners from the dungeon, from the prison those who sit in darkness. (ESV, bold added)

When we devalue Israel, by default, we devalue the Word of God that speaks so highly of them. It is through Israel that we "the nations" have an opportunity to know the LORD.

> Isaiah 43:3, 11
>
> (3) For **I am the LORD** [YHWH; yeh-ho-vaw'] your God, the Holy One of Israel, **your Savior**… (11) I, **I am the LORD, and besides me there is no savior**. (ESV, bold added)

---

99 Genesis 12:3

Digest this theological truth:
Per Isaiah, YHWH is the Savior of Israel.

The historic Catholic Church changed the Sabbath to Sunday. Similarly, today, the pro-abortionist movement has redefined murder. The business world has redefined honesty and integrity. The institutional church has redefined what it means to obey God.

> Acts 17:10-11
> 10 The brothers [and sisters] immediately sent Paul and Silas away by night to Berea, and when they arrived they went into the Jewish synagogue. 11 Now these Jews were more noble than those in Thessalonica; they received the word with all eagerness, examining the Scriptures daily to see if these things were so. (ESV)

The Bereans were Jews. They validated the relevance of Paul's message to the teachings found in the *Tanakh* (Old Testament). In like manner, the words of the New Testament receive its greatest validation from words found in the *Tanakh* (Old Testament).

The Jewishness of the first followers of Christ is revealed in that they celebrated the festivals, honored the Sabbath, followed the dietary regulations, etc. In Acts 3:1, even the times of prayer were still honored. "Now Peter and John were going up to the temple at the hour of prayer, the ninth hour."[100] Even Jesus celebrated *Hanukkah.*

---

100 See Psalm 55:17; Daniel 6:10 for the times of prayer.

John 10:22-23, "At that time the Feast of Dedication [*Hanukkah*] took place at Jerusalem. It was winter, and Jesus was walking in the temple, in the colonnade of Solomon."

This simply validates the grafting of the "nations" into the true vine, Israel. It was well into the second and third centuries before the Jewishness of Jesus and the Jewish practices found among the first Christians started to be challenged in a quantitative way. It was not challenged by the Bible! It was challenged by religious and political leaders. They were the Pharisees and Sadducees of the day.

Fact: Anti-Semitism is synonymous with anti-Judaism and it has a racial (anti-YHWH) root. This anti-Semitic attitude was given more and more life during the ensuing ages. The culmination was Nazi Germany's term, the "Final Solution," which was their plan to annihilate the Jewish people. For the most part, both Catholics and Protestants remained silent as Hitler released his plan to exterminate the Jews from Western Europe. Their silence was in fact an endorsement of this hideous act.

At the stroke of the pen by the Pope, everything the Bible said about the seventh day Sabbath was null and void. We Protestants are like blind sheep following antichrist's message.

History does tell us that many openly opposed this ruling about the Sabbath; not only the Jews. However, Emperor Constantine and the Catholic Church had no problem killing any "Christians" that stood in their way.

A book by Cardinal Gibbons, originally published in 1876, titled *Faith of Our Fathers*, 92nd ed., p. 89, openly states that, "You may read the Bible from Genesis to Revelation, and you will not find a single line authorizing the sanctification of Sunday. The Scriptures enforce the religious observance of Saturday."[101]

I have personally witnessed how angry Christians can get when I share this truth about the Sabbath. Yet, this Catholic Cardinal is just saying what is true according to the Bible: Man changed the Sabbath to Sunday; NOT God! Like it or not, "The Scriptures enforce the religious observance of Saturday" as the true Sabbath. [102]

A few years later, in 1893, Cardinal Gibbons openly wrote that "The Catholic Church … by virtue of her divine mission, changed the day from Saturday to Sunday" (*The Catholic Mirror*, official publication of James Cardinal Gibbons, Sept. 23, 1893).[103]

> Jeremiah 2:13
> "for my people have committed two evils: they *have forsaken me, the fountain of living waters*, **and** *hewed out cisterns for themselves*, broken cisterns that can hold no water." (ESV, italics and bold added)

A cistern was usually man-made and, at times, carved out of solid rock to store water. These people have willingly left God and His Word as their source and the meaning for living life (the living water). These people have made their own source of water; which is not from God. These people have chosen death as opposed to life with God.

---

101 http://cgi.org/who-changed-the-sabbath-to-sunday, accessed August 14, 2017
102 ibid
103 ibid

This assumptive authority, assumed by the Pope and the Catholic Church, is the same "water" (Jeremiah 2:13) that eventually flowed into our Protestant Churches.

Even today we want to have people come to church so that we may convince them to be saved. They must come to us on Sunday! The Church assumed the power to save, or at least, the church inserted itself as a critical component in the salvation journey.

To the degree that this truth about the Sabbath and the Church penetrates your thinking and behavior reveals the depth of the deception in your own life.

It is only when we move into a saving relationship with the Father and Son, do we become a part of the Body of Christ, the congregation of believers, the biblical Church.

This "lie" opened the door for the concept that God's chosen people, the Hebrews, could not be "saved" unless they were baptized by the Church. Even "forced baptisms" (in the opinion of the Pope) "were recognized by God."[104]

Pope Innocent III reigned from AD 1198 until his death in 1216. "Pope Innocent III embraced the title Vicar of Christ (*Vicarious Christi).*" This new title gave the Pope "absolute [spiritual and theological] power."[105]

104 Carroll, *Constantine's Sword*, 275
105 Ibid, 280

Pope Innocent III was one of the three popes to define the doctrine of "no salvation outside the Church,"[106]

This definition of salvation was defined by powerful men; not God. Man defined the meaning of "Church" as an institution controlled by men with religious titles. No longer would the Bible, or even God, define what Church meant.

Question: Can you see how the historic Catholic Church re-defined the manner in which future generations viewed the institution we call Church today?

In a purely biblical sense, the word church may be viewed in three different ways: First, as the body of Christ as viewed as a local assembly or group of believers (1 Corinthians 1:2; 2 Corinthians 1:1; Galatians 1:1-2). Second, it is defined as the individual believer (1 Corinthians 15:9; Galatians 1:13). Third, the believer individually and believers corporately are the Temple of God. The Church is the aggregate Body to whom Jesus has given His life. If you touch a Christian, you have touched Christ's Church (Matthew 9:15; 25:13; Mark 2:19-20; Luke 5:34-35; John 3:29; 2 Corinthians 11:2; Ephesians 5:22-32; Revelation 19:7-9).

The actions of the Catholic Church formalized and centralized the non-biblical institution we know as the church today. The good news is that this man-made model is losing ground as young, new believers see the fallacy of the institution, even if they do not know the history.

---

106 http://catholicism.org/pope-innocent-iii-and-the-marks-of-a-great-papacy.html, accessed August 23, 2017.

This Sunday, you will probably "go to church," which is not the biblical example as the early believers "came together as the church." Plus, they met together almost every day.

The Sunday Visitor is a publishing house that serves the Catholic Church. It was started in 1912. One of its publications made a joke about us Protestants. As printed in 1923 in a publication by the Catholic Church, "Sunday is our mark of authority… the church [the Catholic Church] is above the Bible, and this transference of Sabbath observance is proof of that fact"[107] "Protestants do not realize that by observing Sunday, they accept the authority of … the Pope" (*Our Sunday Visitor*, February 5, 1950). [108]

Call ourselves Protestants all day long, yet when it comes to the Sabbath, we follow the Pope's directive. Allow the previous statement to settle into your mind and heart…by changing the Sabbath, the Catholic Church's authority (in practice) is above the Word of God. At least that is what they thought. Sadly, this attitude of authority is evident in some Protestant churches.

---

107 *Catholic Record of London, Ontario* Sept 1, 1923). (http://cgi.org/who-changed-the-sabbath-to-sunday, accessed August 14, 2017

108 http://cgi.org/who-changed-the-sabbath-to-sunday, accessed August 14, 2017

Ezekiel 22:26

Her priests have done violence to my law and have profaned my holy things. They have made no distinction between the holy and the common, *neither have they taught the difference between the unclean and the clean, and they have disregarded my Sabbaths*, so that I am profaned among them. (ESV, Italics added)

Isaiah 56:1-2

Thus says the LORD: "Keep justice, and do righteousness, for soon my salvation will come, and my righteousness be revealed. Blessed is the man who does this, and the son of man who holds it fast, who *keeps the Sabbath, not profaning it*, and keeps his hand from doing any evil." (ESV, Italics added)

Keeping the Sabbath has nothing to do with one's salvation. It has to do with obedience, like not judging others or not stealing.

Mark 2:27, "And he said to them, "The Sabbath was made for man, not man for the Sabbath." (ESV)

Acts 17:10-11, "The brothers immediately sent Paul and Silas away by night to *Berea*, and when they arrived they went into the *Jewish synagogue*. Now *these Jews were more noble* than those in Thessalonica; they received the word with all eagerness, *examining the Scriptures daily to see if these things were so*." (ESV, Italics added)

"Examining the Scriptures daily" informs us that the Bereans looked into the *Tanakh* (our Old Testament) to prove *all of what Paul was teaching was correct.*

> Colossians 2:13-17
>
> 13 When you were dead in your sins and in the uncircumcision of your flesh, God made you alive with Christ. *He forgave us all our sins, 14 having canceled the charge of our legal indebtedness*, which stood against us and condemned us; he has taken it away, *nailing it to the cross.* 15 And having disarmed the powers and authorities, he made a public spectacle of them, triumphing over them by the cross. 16 *Therefore* do not let anyone judge you by what you eat or drink, or with regard to a religious festival, a New Moon celebration or a Sabbath day. 17 These are a shadow of the things that were to come; the reality, however, is found in Christ (ESV, italics added)

The subject addressed in Colossians 2 is the control that sin had on us *before* we were forgiven. Verse 14 states that the *control of sin has been broken.* It shows that Christ cancelled our debt (the written code about our sin).

In an email I received from a pastor while covering this text, he stated "In Colossians 2:14, what did Jesus nail to the cross? It was the Ten Commandments. The law came to show us our sin and how far away we were from God and Jesus came to make us righteous before Him. Teachings of the bible were clearly wiped away by Jesus." This pastor went on to tell me that Christians today "do not have to follow any of the imperatives found in the Bible."

The statement in Colossians 2 may easily be taken out of context. As with the whole Bible, we need to look at the context of the passage being studied. For example, when we read the word "food" in the New Testament, it means things that are biblically deemed eatable. Unclean animals or unclean fish are never listed as "food." We should not take the word "food" and read it the context of our culture today. To do so gives the reader a false understanding of the true biblical meaning.

Secondly, the "record of debt" has been cancelled. That is to say, the "record of our sins has been thrown out of God's Court."[109] "Because the Messiah died for our sins, this record of our transgressions is inadmissible evidence in the Courtroom of Heaven. Because of the work of our Advocate, Yeshua, we have triumphed over our accuser."[110] In verse 15, since there is no record of our sin, no one can judge us by the things we do or the biblically defined food we eat. The word "therefore" in verse 16 points us back to the previous verses about our sin debt being cancelled, not to redefine what biblical "food" is.

One way we could paraphrase the passage is this: "You have been forgiven. (v.13)"

---

109 Written by Daniel Botkin, http://www.giveshare.org/Health/dietarylaws.html, accessed September 5, 2017.

110 Ibid.

"The record of your sins has been removed from God's Courtroom through the work of your Advocate, Yeshua. (v. 14)"

"He triumphed over your accuser, the devil, so you can be victorious over sin. (v.15)"

[Because Yeshua has prevailed, therefore], "don't give anyone the opportunity to condemn you [about what meat you eat, or what you drink] "or in respect of a holy day, or the new moon, or the sabbath days. In other words, through the Messiah you have the power to obey the commandments of God which regulate these things."

"Therefore walk in obedience so that no man can condemn you for not obeying God's commandments regarding food, drink, holy days, new moon, and sabbaths."

"These things are important because they are shadows [not *were* shadows, but *are* shadows] of things yet to come [not of things that *have already come*]. (v.17)

The above paraphrase *affirms God's dietary laws* rather than abolishing them. Even if someone wants to interpret Col. 2:16 to mean "don't worry about dietary laws," the context forces us to understand this to mean "don't worry about man-made regulations concerning food and drink." The entire passage is dealing with man-made regulations of human origin. [111] ([inserted text] added)

---

111 Ibid.

In Acts 17:10-11, Paul desires the Jews in Berea to walk in freedom and to observe the teaching of the Bible, the *Tanakh*; which they examined to prove what Paul was teaching was accurate.

Verse 13 of Colossians 2 addresses our being dead in our sins *before* we were regenerated by the finished work of Christ. This verse only deals with our obtaining salvation and the forgiveness of sin in that Christ has cancelled our *enslavement to sin* (the power of the Enemy over us) that existed beforehand; *not any of the teachings of the Bible.*

Four general areas are addressed in Colossians 2:16 -

1. food and drink – our diet
2. festival – what festivals we are to celebrate
3. new moon – what calendars or signs of the times should we follow
4. Sabbath – the teachings about Sabbaths (It is God that we obey)

In Colossians 2, another reason we are not concerned with what any person says about what we eat, or how we observe the festivals of the Bible or even the Sabbath is that *GOD has already given His opinion about them.*

Question: When was the first mention of clean and unclean animals in the Bible? (Genesis 7:1, 2)

Genesis 9:3 states that "Every moving thing that lives shall be food for you. And as I gave you the green plants, I give you everything." This passage can easily be taken out of context if read in a literal sense without understanding of earlier texts.

In the context of the Old Testament, once something was declared "unclean," it was never referred to as "food" after that point in time. So, Genesis 9:3 is talking about clean animals.

According to the Bible, "for at least a thousand years before the *Torah* was given to Moses," there existed "a distinction between clean and unclean animals."[112]

As we proceed through the Bible, when meat for food is mentioned, it is already assumed that we are speaking of clean animals. "Genesis does not tell us which animals were clean and which were unclean, but it is obvious that Noah knew the difference."[113] Clean animals are fit for human consumption. Unclean animals are not good for humans to eat.

Although not a part of this study, there are only a few passages in the New Testament that are used to *imply that the dietary laws are no longer in effect* (Matthew 15, Acts 10, Colossians 2, Luke 10 and 1 Corinthians 10). If the whole of the Bible is studied in a biblically, cultural manner, a right conclusion is reached, which is, the dietary laws of the Bible are still in force today.

Were there any "Jews" when Noah entered the ark? Was Noah a Jew? The answer is "No." There were approximately four hundred years from the death of Noah to the call of Abraham.

The descendants of Abraham, Isaac, Jacob, and, in particular, Judah (*Yehudah*) "morphed into an ethno-religious group" called

---

112 Ibid.
113 Ibid.

"Jews." "The original Israelite kingdom was called Judah. During the Persian Period the land became a province of that empire, called *Yehud*; then in the Roman Period, the land became a Roman province called *Judea*."[114]

When we look back at our Patriarchs, remember that the Matriarchs were all barren. Sarah, Rebecca and Rachel were all unable to bare children until God intervened. Through these men and women God introduced the DNA of the Jewish people. Regardless of your personal opinion or theology, Israel (the Jewish people) is special to YHWH [yeh-ho-vaw']. On our best day, we Gentiles are grafted into them. Never forget this!

The event of Genesis 7 mentions "clean" and "unclean" animals, which predates the laws of Moses. Keep in mind Exodus 15:26.

> "If you will diligently listen to the voice of the LORD your God, and do that which is right in his eyes, and give ear to his commandments and keep all his statutes, I will put none of the diseases on you that I put on the Egyptians, for I am the LORD, your healer." (ESV)

If following the dietary guidelines of the Bible will keep me healthy, I'm in!

An article I recently read brings a new concern to the expression "clean meat."

---

[114] http://www.haaretz.com/jewish/archaeology/1.681177, accessed September 13, 2017.

> Billionaire Richard Branson and Microsoft founder Bill Gates have invested in a startup working to create meat that doesn't involve killing animals. Memphis Meats makes synthetic beef, chicken, and duck "from self-producing animal cells," citing the rising demand from consumers for organic protein that is "less reliant on feed, land, and water." The products are not yet commercially available, but have attracted investments from big agricultural companies like Cargill. Branson predicts that in 30 years, "all meat will either be clean or plant-based." Other agricultural companies that are investing in the "clean meat" movement include Tyson Foods, which has invested in Beyond Meta, another synthetic meat company.[115]

Question: Haven't Gentile Christians been called to enjoy the liberty we have in Christ, therefore, we are no longer bound to the teachings of the Old Testament; the Law?

Our modern Western values equate "freedom in Christ" with doing whatever we want. (Sounds like Greek thinking to me.) God calls us to a higher standard. As noted in Colossians 2:16, we are not to allow the opinions of people to over-ride the Word. Jesus tells us that "If you love me, you will keep my commandments." (John 14:15, ESV). His commandments are not arbitrary dos and don'ts that may vary from church to church. Nor are they the imperatives of the Bible that we select *a la carte*. No, His commandments are the imperatives of the whole Bible. Extreme care is to be exercised in deciding that a particular imperative is no longer active today.

115 THE WEEK, September 8, 2017 issue, page 18.

1 Peter 1:11

"They wondered what time or situation the Spirit of Christ within them was talking about when he told them in advance about Christ's suffering and his great glory afterward." (NLT)[116]

In 1 Peter 1:11 we are informed that "the Spirit of Christ" was in the prophets of the Old Testament. Therefore, we can correctly say that it was Christ that authored, thus established the imperatives found in the Old Testament. Christ is the Word that became flesh (John 1:14).

Always let the Word of God make the decisions as to what the Bible actually says; not anyone or anything else. Be like the Jews in Berea and prove the New Testament with the words from the Old Testament!

2 Timothy 2:15

Do your best to present yourself to God as one approved, a worker who does not need to be ashamed and who correctly handles the word of truth. (NIV)

Daniel 7:25

"He shall speak words against the Most High, **and** shall wear out the saints of the Most High, **and** shall think *to change the times and the law*; **and** they shall be given into **his** hand for a time, times, and half a time." (ESV, italics and bold added)

116 NLT - Scripture quotations are taken from the Holy Bible, *New Living Translation*, copyright ©1996, 2004, 2007. Used by permission of Tyndale House Publishers, Inc., Carol Stream, Illinois 60188. All Rights Reserved.

Deception #1 - The Authority of the Institutional Church

It was the Pope's declaration and NOT the Bible that changed the Sabbath from Saturday to Sunday. With the focus on the institutional Church as the only avenue for salvation, in the eyes of some Western Christian, *the Church's authority is above the Bible.*

The Catholic Church with the attitude that her doctrine is the only right doctrine is evident today in our Western Churches.

CHAPTER SIX

Deception #2

The Sabbath has been replaced with Sunday, a Pagan day of worship

Psalm 55:17

Evening and morning and at noon I utter my complaint and moan, and he will hear my voice. (NRSV, italics added)

Daniel 6:10

Although Daniel knew that the document had been signed, he continued to go to his house, which had windows in its upper room open toward Jerusalem, and to get down on his knees *three times a day to pray to his God and praise him, just as he had done previously*. (NRSV, italics added)

For centuries, Christians' celebration of Easter was on Passover, and the observance of the Sabbath was on Saturday (the seventh day of the week). As we now know, this was all changed by Constantine and the historic Catholic Church. Even the observance of the historically established times of prayer was forgotten. Why?

As anti-Semitism and anti-Judaism gained more and more ground, the Anti-Messiah (aka antichrist) (1 John 2:18) did everything in its power to remove any hint of the practices of the *Tanakh* from the growing non-Jewish Church. Anti-Messiah wanted to remove YHWH (the God of Abraham, Isaac, and Jacob) from the operation of the emerging Catholic Church in order to direct attention away from *Adonai* and His chosen people. (When YHWH is read from Scripture, Hebrews say *Adonai.*)

Emperor Constantine lived from AD 272 to 337. During this period of time the first day of the week, Sunday, was the official day of rest in the Roman Empire.

Trivia: *Hellenism* is the term used to describe the influence of Greek culture on the people living in either the Greek or Roman Empires. When Alexander the Great extended his territory from Greece into Egypt and as far east as India, the influence of the Greek culture and language soon followed. The Roman Empire continued what Alexander started. The influence of the Greek and Roman cultures is referred to as *Hellenization.*

Astrology entered the Rome Empire through Hellenization. So many people were involved with astrology that the expression "Chaldean wisdom" became the synonym of divination through the planets and stars.[117]

Astrology, at its center, was the physical sun. Those involved in astrology saw the sun as the "source of eternal life, and believed that the Sun was the manifestation of God."[118] That God was revealed through the physical sun.

---

117 Parker, Derek and Julia, 1983. *A history of Astrology* (Harper Collins Distribution Services: Deutsch, 1983), 16.

118 https://www.astrotheme.com/files/history_of_astrology.php, accessed September 5, 2017.

Astrology is, of course, demonic at its core in the sense that it causes people to look to some other source for Divine guidance than the God of Abraham, Isaac and Jacob.

A study of history reveals the deception of un-biblical authority, exercised by the institution called the Church, when it changed the Sabbath to Sunday. Speaking of the Sabbath, in Genesis 2:2, what did it mean for God to end "*His work and He rested*"?

> Genesis 2:2, 3
> "And on the seventh day God *ended His work* which He had done, *and He rested* on the seventh day from all His work which He had done. Then God blessed the seventh day and sanctified it, because in it He rested from all His work which God had created and made." (NKJV, Italics added)

The Hebrew word translated "ended His work" in verse 2 comes from the Hebrew root *shabat* (English "Sabbath"). *Shabat* became the official name for the seventh day of the week. The word "sanctified" in verse 3 comes from the root *qadash*, which literally means "to set apart as holy." For us, as with saints of old, Sabbath is one day that is to be set aside as a day to rest from normal activities that occurred the previous six days. It is a day to reflect upon what God (YHWH[119]) has done in our lives the previous six days.

119 (Sometimes written as YHVH.) This is known as the tetragrammaton (meaning consisting of "four letters"). YHWH is the four-letter biblical name of God. The tetragrammaton consists of four Hebrew letters: *yod, heh, waw*, and then *heh*. Although some versions of the Bible translate the tetragrammaton as "*Yahweh*" or "*Jehovah*", *Yahweh* may be more accurate. Most translate it as "LORD" (all capital letters).

God was not tired in that he needed to rest due to exhaustion. Basically, God ceased from His creative activities. For us humans (who do get tired), we need a day for rest. Due to both misunderstanding of what Sabbath biblically means, coupled with man's attempt to override what God established (both by the Catholic Church and rabbinic teachings), we Gentiles believers openly disobey God's commandment about observing the Sabbath. After all, the "church" has told us our whole lives that Sunday (the first day of the week) is the official day of rest. (Emperor Constantine would be pleased with us!)

We need to be careful to pay attention to what we have heard or been taught about the Sabbath. Why? It was most likely taught that observing the Sabbath was part of the Law! Really? What Law do we mean?

If we read Exodus 20:2-17 or Deuteronomy 5:6-21, we see that God commanded His followers:

1. You shall have no other gods before Me.

    - If you recall one of the differences between biblical thinking and Greek thinking is that to the Hebrew, God is in the center of his or her world; not self.
    - In the final version of the Declaration of Independence the words express a core cultural value of the United States; "We hold these truths to be self-evident, that all men are created equal, that they are endowed by their Creator with certain unalienable Rights, that among these are Life, Liberty and the pursuit of Happiness."

Often, in our "pursuit of Happiness" God is removed from the equation. It becomes all about my happiness. Therefore, the end result is that self has replaced God as the center of our lives.

2. You shall make no idols.

> An idol is something that rules us and makes us a slave. Whatever challenges Jesus' right [to rule] in our hearts becomes His enemy. An idol is not occasional sin; it is something that rules us and makes us a slave. Whatever challenges Jesus' right in our hearts becomes His enemy, which He will confront. You may feel you are not worshiping any idols. You may not stand, morning by morning, before a statue of Baal and praise it as your God. Indeed, we do not worship the idols of the ancient heathen. Like everything in a modern world, man has sophisticated idolatry as well. The spirit of antichrist is that spirit which exalts *self* as *deity*. You see, the spirit of antichrist is much more subtle than someone suddenly announcing to the world he is the Creator. For us today, we must look for the influence of antichrist in our religious traditions: are those traditions founded upon Scripture or upon man?[120]

3. You shall not take the name of the Lord your God in vain.

   - ❑ Because of this command, Jewish people will not even write the letters GOD. They write G_d. When YHWH is read from Scripture, they say *Adonai*.

120 Frangipane, *Holiness, Truth and the Presence of God*, 79-80

4. **Keep the Sabbath day holy.**

    - Sabbath, according to the Bible, is the seventh day of the week. God never changed this day to the first day of the week.
    - To NOT honor the Sabbath, by your actions, you have in essence removed this command from the Bible!

5. Honor your father and your mother.

    - We do this by showing respect, not so much for whom or what the parent has, or has not, done. Rather, we honor them because God has commanded us to do so. This command requires us to engage in action towards our parents. This, I feel, should extend to all parental figures in our lives.

6. You shall not murder.

    - Based upon the number of abortions in the USA, we ignore this command too.
    - The top reasons babies are killed (aborted):
        - 19% of the women do not want any more children;
        - 23% say they can't afford a baby;
        - 25% are not ready for a child.
    - Do you see the Greek/Western mindset being used?
    - Who is in the center of their lives, God or self?

7. You shall not commit adultery.

- "Among born-again Christians, an extremely high 95 percent say that they have looked at pornography, with 54 percent indicating that they view it at least on a monthly basis and 44 percent admitting that they saw it at work within the past three months."[121]
- "You adulterous people! Do you not know that friendship with the world is enmity with God? Therefore whoever wishes to be a friend of the world makes himself an enemy of God" (ESV). Based on James 4:4, we commit spiritual adultery by being overly influenced by the values and systems of this world.
- We are quick to observe cultural holidays, yet we do not think twice about ignoring the biblical holidays. [122]
- When we fail to obey God's Word, on some level we have allowed something other than the Word to govern our lives, which, by definition is spiritual adultery.

---

121 https://www.onenewsnow.com/culture/2014/10/09/survey-alarming-rate-of-christian-men-look-at-porn-commit-adultery, accessed October 20, 2017.

122 Although not listed specifically as one of the *End Time Deceptions*, I have started to study these biblical feasts. Why? The Bible says that the seven holidays are literally "the feasts of the LORD" (Lev. 23:4). "God instituted only seven holidays (or holydays)." These appointed times belong to God. He gave instructions to us about them, and, as with the seventh day Sabbath, He has not called an end to them being observed. These feasts are "intended to be times" for us to meet God "for holy purposes." [Kevin Howard, Marvin Rosenthal, *The Feats of the Lord* (Nashville, TN: Thomas Nelson, 1997), 13.]

8. You shall not steal.

- An "unbelievable 30 percent of all workers will steal"[123] from their employers and others.

9. You shall not bear false witness against your neighbor.

- "John Wesley said bearing false witness is 'speaking falsely in any matter' including 'lying, equivocating, and any way devising and designing to deceive our neighbour,' or to speak 'unjustly against our neighbour, to the prejudice of his reputation.' Of course it's not always that men are out to ruin another's reputation, but they care nothing of ruining another's reputation in the pursuit of making their point." [124]

10. You shall not covet.

    a. This command involves an action within one's thoughts. When we break this command we are operating contrary to the command to "love your neighbor as yourself."

By the way, NONE of these commandments have expired!

---

123 Based upon data from Brotherhood Mutual and Church Mutual insurance companies and Frank Sommerville, JD, CPA. https://www.sharefaith.com/blog/2015/09/18-church-embezzlement, accessed October 20, 2017.

124 http://www.christianitytoday.com/edstetzer/2008/december/bearing-false-witness.html, October 20, 2017.

Remember that it was God who gave us these commandments. It is not some nebulous "law" that has been replaced by grace. Grace preceded these commands. Be careful, deception is like poison that has no taste or smell, yet, it is nonetheless poison to your soul. "Yes, I know that these laws of God do not align with our cultural, Western values."[125] Never forget that God made these rules!

> Ezekiel 11:12
>
> "Then you shall know that I am the Lord, *whose statutes you have not followed, and whose ordinances you have not kept*, but *you have acted according to the ordinances of the nations that are around you*." (NRSV, italics added)

As followers of the LORD God and His Son, we should be out-of-step with the world and the society in which we live. We should not conform to religious practices that do not 100% align with the Bible. Our goal is conformity to the Word of God and not to the dreams and values of the Western world.

> 2 Corinthians 6:14-18
>
> 14 Be ye not unequally yoked together with unbelievers: for what fellowship hath righteousness with unrighteousness? and what communion hath light with darkness? 15 And what concord hath Christ with Belial? or what part hath he that believeth with an infidel? 16 And what agreement hath the

125 CBJ, *Complete Jewish Bible*, Copyright © 1998 by David H. Stern. All rights reserved.

> temple of God with idols? for ye are the temple of the living God; as God hath said, I will dwell in them, and walk in them; and I will be their God, and they shall be my people. 17
> *Wherefore come out from among them, and be ye separate, saith the Lord, and touch not the unclean thing; and I will receive you.* 18 And will be a Father unto you, and ye shall be my sons and daughters, saith the Lord Almighty. (KJV, italics added)

Regarding the Sabbath, of course, over the years many a well-intended rabbi or religious leader added to the traditional laws governing the Sabbath, but these are not God's laws. If we take one step away from allowing the teaching of the whole Bible to be the benchmark for living, we enter into a very dangerous place.

To cease from doing things on the Sabbath does not mean to stop doing everything! Even on the Sabbath we may be just as busy as any other day, however; we should not be engaged in activities as we normally do the other six days. Sabbath should include time to enjoy God and His blessings.

The fourth commandment tells us to rest from our normal daily activities so we may spend time doing what we enjoy. You may have heard that, as Christians, "every day is holy." If this is the case, then what makes the Sabbath special?

Colossians 2:8, 16

(8) See to it that no one takes you captive through philosophy and empty deception, which are based on human tradition and the spiritual forces of the world rather than on Christ. (BSB[126])

(16) Therefore do not let anyone condemn you in matters of food[127] and drink or of observing festivals, new moons, or sabbaths. (NRS)

Based upon these passages, it is between you, the Bible and God as to what is permissible for you to do on the Sabbath. The clear requirements from Scripture are to make a distinction between the seventh day and the other six days.

In Romans 3:20, Paul says, "Therefore, no one will be declared righteous in his sight by observing the law". In Romans 7:12, Paul declares, "So then, the law is holy, and the commandment is holy, righteous and good."

What is important, based upon other Scriptures we have already covered, is that the Ten Commandments play no role in our salvation; however, we will obey them **because** of our relationship

---

126 (BSB) *The Berean Bible* © 2016 by Bible Hub and Berean. Bible. Used by Permission. All rights Reserved.

127 God does not change (Numbers 23:19; Hebrews 13:8; James 1:17). Therefore, God's Word does not change (John 1:14). Yes, the Western theological world, at times, treats the Bible as if God's Word does change; which is not true. Therefore, just as murder or stealing should be defined by the Bible and not one's culture, the same is true for words like food. The word "food" has been defined in the Bible; therefore, culture should not override its biblical meaning. Since God gives only good things (James 1:17) to His people, which is validated in Romans 7:12, "the law is holy, and the commandment holy and just and good", we know that His Word, with all of its commands, is for our benefit.

with the Father, Son and Holy Spirit. The cause-effect should not be confusing to us. We have been redeemed (the cause), therefore we obey the Bible (the effect).

Remember Matthew 7:21: "*Not everyone who says to me, 'Lord, Lord,' will enter the kingdom of heaven*, but the *one who does the will of my Father who is in heaven*" (italics added). The Ten Commandments are part of the "will" of the "Father".

Daniel 9:4, "I prayed to the LORD my God and made confession, saying, 'O Lord, the great and awesome God, *who keeps covenant and steadfast love with those who love him and keep his commandments*'" (ESV, italics added).

We cannot separate loving God from obeying the commands in the Bible and remain biblically correct. Daniel clarifies this in verse 5 (and verse 10), "*we have sinned and done wrong and acted wickedly and rebelled, turning aside from your commandments and rules* (ESV, italics added).

Obedience is required, even when we do not agree with the imperative. Luke 5:5, And Simon answered, "Master, we toiled all night and took nothing! But at your word I will let down the nets." (ESV) We obey because the LORD said for us to obey.

Do the Ten Commandments save us? No!

Are they relevant for us today? Yes!

On the Sabbath, we rest from our regular work and we rest in the finished work of Jesus.

Deception #2 - The Sabbath day changed to Sunday. The Word of God that teaches us to observe the seventh day, the Sabbath has been replaced with a pagan day of worship.

CHAPTER SEVEN

Deception #3

The arrangement of the Bible changed

> Our English Bibles follow the order as given in the Latin Vulgate. This order, therefore, depends on the arbitrary judgment of one man, Jerome. All theories based on this order rest on human authority, and are thus without any true foundation.[128]
>
> All the teachings in the Bible become clearer and plainer when the Biblical books are placed back in their correct order. It is truly amazing what the books of the Bible have to tell us when we read the Holy Scriptures in the context that was first intended by God and those who officially canonized the Bible.[129]

Turn to the front of your Bible at the table of contents. Look at the order of the Books in the Old Testament. Do you notice anything wrong? (Probably not.) Why, because this is the arrangement we have always known. Yet, it is not the order that God had established or the order the Messiah would recognize.

---

128 E.W. Bullinger, *The Companion Bible* (Grand Rapids, Michigan: Zondervan Bible Publishers, 1974), 139 (Appendix).

129 Earnest Martin, *Restoring the Original Bible*, (Ann Arbor, Michigan: ASK Publications, 1994), 6.

Daniel 7:25

"He shall *speak words against the Most High*, **and** shall wear out *the saints of the Most High*, **and** shall think *to change the times and the law*; **and** they shall be given into **his** hand for a *time, times, and half a time*." (ESV, italics and bold added)

As we shall see, in about 20 years after Sunday (the first day of the week) was declared the new "Lord's Day" by a man, the Pope, the historical order of the books of the Bible was changed. That's right! When Jerome compiled the Latin Vulgate version of the Bible, the prophecy of Daniel 7:25 ("think to change the times and the law") was fulfilled in part: The official day for the Sabbath was changed *and* the order of the books of the Bible was rearranged.

Eusebius Hieronymus Sophronius was known as Jerome. He was born in AD 345 and became secretary to Pope Damasus in AD 382. "Jerome had been commissioned by Pope Damasus to revise the Old Latin text of the four Gospels from the best Greek texts. The Vulgate is usually credited to have been the first translation of the Old Testament into Latin directly from the Hebrew *Tanakh*, rather than the Greek Septuagint." Between the years AD "390 to 405 A.D. St. Jerome translated…all 39 books in the Hebrew Bible."[130]

It is interesting to note that other writings were part of the official Latin Vulgate Bible (the Book of Baruch,[131] 1 Maccabees and 2

130 http://vulgate.org, accessed October 2, 2017.

131 *Book of Baruch* - Baruch ben Neriah, Jeremiah's scribe

Maccabees,[132] 3 Esdras and 4 Esdras[133], the Prayer of Manasses[134], Laodiceans[135], et al). Do you see these books in your Bible? Why not?

The Vulgate is a Latin version of the Holy Bible, and largely the result of the work of Jerome, who was commissioned by Pope Damasus I in AD 382 to make revisions of the old Latin translations.

Jerome, in a letter to the Pope Damasus dated AD 383, stated that "You urge me to revise the old Latin version, and, as it were, to sit in judgment on the copies of the Scriptures which are now scattered throughout the whole world; and, inasmuch as they differ from one another, you would have me decide which of them agree with the Greek original."[136]

Did you catch the subtle flaws in Jerome's statement above? Who would decide which documents to retain? (Jerome would decide.) And which documents "agree with the Greek original." It is generally accepted today that most, if not all of the Bible was originally in Hebrew or Aramaic, with very little, if any, in Greek. It is unlikely that Jerome had any of the original documents.

---

132 1 and 2 Maccabees - Focuses on the Maccabean Revolt against Antiochus IV Epiphanes and concludes with the defeat of the Syrian general Nicanor in 161 BC by Judas Maccabeus.

133 3 Esdras and 4 Esdras - 1 Esdras is the Book of Ezra. 2 Esdras is the Book of Nehemiah. 3 Esdras and 4 Esdras are separate books.

134 The Prayer of Manasses - The fourth-century Vulgate included it at the end of the book of 2 Chronicles. It later became part of the Matthew Bible and the Geneva Bible of 1599. It is also found in the Apocrypha of the King James Bible.

135 Epistle to the Laodiceans – This is a possible lost letter of Paul the Apostle, the original existence of which is inferred from an instruction to the church in Colossae to send their letter to the church in Laodicea

136 St. Jerome, *The Sacred Writings of St. Jerome*, Translated by William Henry Fremantle (1831-1916) and Philip Schaff (1819-1893), (Jazzybee Verlag: North Charleston, SC, 2017), 519.

Jerome also states that "Matthew the Apostle, who was the first to commit to writing the Gospel of Christ, and who published his work in Judaea in Hebrew characters. We must confess that as we have it in our language (Greek) it is marked by discrepancies".[137] (Discrepancies being defined in that they did not align with the doctrine of the Catholic Church.)

Jerome presents his qualification to correct the "discrepancies" in existing texts by stating that he is a "Christian, born of Christian parents, who carry the standard of the cross on my brow".[138]

It would have been good if he had qualified or quantified what being a "Christian" meant to him, but he did not. What role did his parents play in his own relationship with God is not explained either.

What is for sure is that this task was not the result of Divine revelation. The Pope, not the LORD, has so ordered the rearranging of the Word of God. The historical order of the books of the Bible was changed and the average church member does not know it, and in most cases, is unconcerned by the whole affair.

> "All the Versions, even the Peshito Syriac, the language in which the Gospel is said to have been originally written, conform to the present Greek text. All the quotations of the early writers are from the Greek copy…It should be further noted that although so many of the early writers assert that Matthew originally wrote his Gospel in Hebrew, yet we do not find that any of them ever used it or saw it. Hence if there ever was a Hebrew copy, it must have

137 http://vulgate.org, accessed August 14, 2017

138 Karen Louise Jolly, *Tradition & Diversity, Christianity in a World Context to 1500*, (Routedge: New York, 1997, 2015), 104.

> been lost very early, soon after the destruction of Jerusalem…"[139]
>
> *Peshito* (pəshēt'tä) is the standard translation of the Old and New Testaments in ancient Syriac (sɪri,æk), which is an Aramaic dialect that became the literary and liturgical language of the ancient Syrian Christian churches; the Church of the East as opposed to the Western Roman Catholic Church. In my opinion, the conflict between the East and the West is the longest running Cold War. These two sides have serious differences of opinion about what original language in which the New Testament was written, and which historic documents are authentic. It is important also that one manuscript of the *Peshitta* has a written date corresponding to AD 459/460, "making it the oldest Bible manuscript with a definite date." In 1892, a lady named Agnes Smith Lewis, while searching in a closet in the monastery of St. Catherine in Egypt "an almost complete Syriac codex (kō,deks) of the four Gospels! Scholars now believe that this codex was written in the late fourth century."[140]

It is important to note that Jerome states that "many of the early writers assert that Matthew originally wrote his Gospel in Hebrew". [141]

> Among the four Gospels, which are the only indisputable ones in the Church of God under heaven, I have learned by tradition that the first was written by Matthew, who was once a publican, but afterwards an apostle of Jesus Christ, and it was

[139] Clark, George W., *Notes on the Gospel of Matthew; Explanatory and Practical*, Sheldon and Company, 1870, x

[140] *The Syriac Peshitta—A Window on the World of Early Bible Translations*, https://www.jw.org/en/publications/magazines/wp20140901/syriac-peshitta, accessed October 2, 2017.

[141] Clark, *Notes on the Gospel of Matthew; Explanatory and Practical*, x

> prepared for the converts from Judaism and published in the Hebrew language.[142]
>
> Eusebius himself declared that "Matthew had begun by preaching to the Hebrews, and when he made up his mind to go to others too, he committed his own Gospel to writing in his native tongue [Aramaic], so that for those with whom he was no longer present the gap left by his departure was filled by what he wrote."[143]

Keep in mind that many of the early Western Church leaders did NOT read or speak Hebrew, therefore; the Bible written in Hebrew would be of little use or value to them. This is evident in that the Aramaic and Hebraic idioms are translated literally revealing a lack of understanding of the culture of the original writers. Also, anti-Semitic views would circumvent any desire to be objective about challenging the established status quo views of the Catholic Church. In addition, the intense persecution of the Jews greatly disrupted any historical documents held in Jerusalem, especially around the time the Temple was destroyed.

Jerome states that the Greek copies were filled with errors. Yet, one man, because the Pope had requested it, undertook the task of translating most of the Bible into Latin. "The Catholic Church affirmed the Vulgate as its official Latin Bible at the Council of Trent (1545–

142 *Commentaries on Matthew* [cited by Eusebius in *History of the Church* 6:25] as quoted on https://www.catholic.com/qa/was-matthews-gospel-first-written-in-aramaic-or-hebrew, accessed December 31, 2017.

143 *History of the Church 3:24 [inter 300-325]).* as quoted on https://www.catholic.com/qa/was-matthews-gospel-first-written-in-aramaic-or-hebrew, accessed December 31, 2017.

63)."[144] The Clementine edition of the Vulgate of 1592 became the standard Bible text of the Roman Rite of the Roman Catholic Church and remained so until 1979.

> "It has been considered a strong objection to the Hebrew original of this gospel, that no person, whose writings have come down to us, has intimated that he had ever seen it; and from the earliest times it seems to have existed in the Greek language. But this fact is perfectly consistent with the supposition now made; for the desolation of Judea, and dispersion of the Jewish Christians, having taken place within a few years after the publication of Matthew's gospel, the copies of the original Hebrew would be confined to the Jewish converts; and as other Christians had copies in the Greek, of equal authenticity with the Hebrew, no inquiries would be made after the latter.[145]
>
> As we know, the Bible contains 66 books (39 in the Old Testament and 27 in the New Testament). "While there is no doubt or question that the Bible is complete, the entire Word of God, nevertheless there is a question about the actual number of books and their arrangement or order. Would God design His Word with the mark of man on it? Six is the mark of man."[146]
>
> While the *Tanakh* was written largely in Hebrew, most of the early manuscripts of the New Testament are in

---

144 Bruce M. Metzger, *The Early Versions of the New Testament*, (Clarendon Press: Oxford 1977), 348.

145 Alexander, Archibald, *The Canon of the Old and New Testaments Ascertained, or the Bible Complete Without the Apocrypha and Unwritten Traditions*, (Princeton Press: New York, 1851), 154-164

146 *The Inspired Order of the Bible*, Dr. Judd W. Patton, http:jpatton.bellevue.edu/inspired.html, accessed August 12, 2017

> [koine] Greek…Nevertheless, there is good reason to think that several of the books of the New Testament were written in either Hebrew or Aramaic [a related Semitic language], or drew upon source material in those languages…Moreover, Sha'ul [Paul], whose letters were [perhaps] composed in Greek, clearly drew on his native Jewish and Hebraic thought-forms when he wrote. In fact, some phrases in the New Testament manuscripts make no sense unless one reaches through Greek to the underlying Hebrew expressions. Here is an example, only one of many. Yeshua says in the Sermon on the Mount [Matthew 5-7], literally, "If your eye be evil, your whole body will be dark" [Matthew 6:23]. What is an evil eye? … in Hebrew, having an *'ayin ra'ah,* means being stingy; while having an *'ayin tovah,* a "good eye," means being generous. Yeshua is simply urging generosity against stinginess. And this understanding fits with the surrounding verses: "Where your wealth is, there your heart will be also…You can't be a slave to both God and money." [Matthew 6:21, 24].[147]
>
> Koine Greek (Greek for "common") is a term that came to designate that broad, common form of mostly non-literary Greek used by Greeks in common speech among themselves and with other ethnicities, and used by various ethnicities in their communication with other ethnicities. I find it commonly used as a technical term for a period in history roughly designating the 1st century BCE and CE (BC and AD). But it covers the early centuries of Christian development.[148]

The number six stands for man and human weakness; the evils of Satan and the manifestation of sin. Man was created on the sixth day. Men

147 *The Complete Jewish Bible*, xxxi.

148 http://orvillejenkins.com/languages/koinegreek.html, accessed December 31, 2017.

are appointed 6 days to labor. A Hebrew slave was to serve six years and be released in the 7th year (Jeremiah 34:14). Six years were appointed for the land to be sown and harvested. The number 6 is also associated with Satan in his temptation of Jesus. Number 6 is also used when referring to (human labor) or (secular completeness). The number six is also attached when describing the constant battle between man's spirit and flesh.

The number 66 refers to secular or idol worship as established by humans. The number 66 also deals with any type of falsehood or deception.[149]

The bringing together of three 6's is the number and mark of the Beast of Revelation. As such, **it represents the very best system of governance that mankind can produce without God** and under the constant influence of his chief adversary. Man's system on earth is made up of three parts (economic, religious and governmental) all of which are influenced and led by Satan.[150]

The number 6, in particular the number 66, "amplifies the element of man, seems, therefore, an unlikely number of books for God to include in His Word." To change the number of books in the Bible to 66 may point us to the possible problem. "The evidence from the Bible itself is that there are in fact forty-nine books of the Bible arranged in seven divisions." It does not seem that any Scripture was lost, or added, however; the "most dramatic concern is that many of the books of the Bible have been 'scrambled,' so to speak, from the

---

149 *The Inspired Order of the Bible*, Dr. Judd W. Patton, http:jpatton.bellevue.edu/inspired.html, accessed August 12, 2017

150 Ibid.

order or arrangement as originally canonized and seen in the earliest manuscripts."[151]

> Daniel 7:25
>
> He shall speak words against the Most High, and shall wear out the saints of the Most High, and shall think *to change the times and the law...*

The word *torah* is the Hebrew word for teaching and giving direction for life. Often, English translations use the word "law" instead of "teaching."

> The Hebrew word תורה (torah, Strong's #8451) is usually translated into the English word "Law". Because of this translation there is a great misunderstanding of what "Torah" truly is. "TORAH IS NOT LAW". When we use the word "law" we assume a certain meaning and concept of the word that is not present in the Hebrew Scriptures... The word Torah comes from the Hebrew root word תורה (Y.R.H, Strong's #8451), a verb which means "to flow or throw something"... A Hebraic definition of Torah is "a set of Instructions, from a father to his children. The purpose of a parents Torah is to teach and bring the children to maturity.[152]
>
> "The contemporary arrangement of the Bible is the *Traditional Order* and the original God-ordained order as the *Inspired Order*" (Italics added).[153]

---

151 Ibid.

152 http://www.ancient-hebrew.org/articles_torah.html, accessed August 30, 2017

153 Ibid

> The man most responsible for what became our traditional Bible of sixty-six books was the Catholic theologian, Jerome. His Latin Vulgate translation, written between A.D. 382 and 405, with his "new" arrangement of the books for both the Old and New Testaments, became the standard for Protestant scholars and translators. Once a tradition becomes established, it is difficult to change. Yet Jerome knew better. He had a rationale, a wrong rationale, for making these changes! Regardless, the Tradition lives on today. [154]

The logic of deception:

If you keep repeating a lie long enough, people will believe it is true.

> "Our English Bibles follow the order as given in the Latin Vulgate. This order, therefore, depends on the arbitrary judgment of one man, Jerome. All theories based on this order rest on human authority, and are thus without any true foundation."[155]

While Judaism and a very few English translations of the Bible did not change the arrangement of the books, almost all of Christianity did change the arrangement. Because of Jerome and the Catholic Church, we Protestant Christians do not use the original book order and very few of us even know it! The order of the books in the Bible, especially the *Tanakh*, was firmly established and used in the first century by Jesus and His early followers. Who is man that he should tamper with such sacred documents?

---

154 ibid

155 Martin, *Restoring the Original Bible*, 20.

> Luke 24:44-45
>
> Then he said to them, "These are my words that I spoke to you while I was still with you, that everything written about me in the **Law of Moses** and the **Prophets** and the **Psalms** must be fulfilled." Then he opened their minds to understand the Scriptures (the *Tanakh*). (ESV, bold added)

In Luke 24, Jesus, not Jerome or the Pope, validated the right order for the Bible: **Law of Moses**, the **Prophets**, and the **Psalms**. Jesus used the word Psalms to refer "to the Writings section, which in the *Tanakh* begins with the Psalms, not Job".[156]

The three divisions of the Hebrew Scriptures:

1. The **Law** (The Five Books of Moses, called the *Chumash*. Also called the ***Torah****, which means teaching.* Also called the *Pentateuch*[157])
2. The **Prophets (*Nevi'im)***
3. The **Writings (Psalms) (*Ketuvim)***.

> Romans 3:2
>
> Much in every way. To begin with, the Jews were entrusted with the oracles [revelations; words] of God. (ESV)

God's chosen people, Israel, was given the task to preserve the original twenty-four books/scrolls.

---

156 *The Complete Jewish Bible*, xxvii.

157 The word *Pentateuch* comes from a combination of the Greek word *penta*, meaning "five" and *teuchos*, which can be translated "scroll."

> Hebrew Bible is a term describing the common portions of the Jewish and Christian biblical canons. The term is considered neutral and is preferred in academic writing and interfaith settings over "Old Testament," which hints at the Christian doctrine of supersessionism, in which the "old" covenant of God with the Jews has been made obsolete by the "new" covenant with the Christians. The Jewish term for the Hebrew Bible is "Tanakh," a Hebrew acronym its component parts: the Torah, Prophets, and Writings.[158]

The word ***TaNaKh***, in fact is an acronym based on the initial Hebrew letters of each of the text's three parts: [159]

1. ***Torah* means "instruction."** Also called the "Pentateuch" or the "Books of Moses." This part of the *Tanakh* follows the same order and division of books adopted in the Christian version.
    - **Five books**: Genesis, Exodus, Leviticus, Numbers and Deuteronomy

2. ***Nevi'im*, meaning "Prophets**." The Jewish tradition includes the "historical" books of Joshua, Kings and Samuel in this category.
    - **Eight Books of the *Nevi'im***: Joshua, Judges, Samuel, Kings, Isaiah, Jeremiah, Ezekiel, and The Twelve (one book for the minor prophets)

---

158 http://www.newworldencyclopedia.org/entry/Hebrew_Bible, accessed August 15, 2017

159 ibid

3. ***Ketuvim*, meaning "Writings"** (Called "Psalms" by Jesus in Luke 24:44). These include **Eleven Books**:
   - historical writings (Ezra/Nehemiah and the Book of Chronicles)
   - wisdom books (Job, Ecclesiastes and Proverbs)
   - poetry (Psalms, Lamentations and the Song of Solomon)
   - biographies (Ruth, Esther and Daniel)

Deception #3 - Reordering the arrangement of the Bible

Changing the order of the Bible to satisfy man's desire over the historically accepted order for God's Word should not be taken lightly.

Daniel 7:25, fulfilled in part, *changing of order of the Word* (the *Tanakh*).

CHAPTER EIGHT

Deception #4

My hands are clean as I stand before the LORD

> The cohesion of a given language and culture forces the Western reader of the Bible to lay aside our familiar and usual cultural lens of our language and its cultural bent and look anew at the Scriptures. As we do so, we need to use care in how we understand the terminologies and imperatives of the whole Bible. One way to express this is expressed in the following quote: Demonstrating our faith through obedience to God's word believing everything laid down in the Torah and prophets; we believe that the commandments are a guardrail to protect us, not a fence to restrict us. We do not teach that we follow Torah FOR salvation; we follow it BECAUSE OF our salvation and faith in its Author.[160]

We have covered three primary deceptions of the End Time. Here is a brief summary:

Deception #1. The Authority of the Institutional Church - The Sabbath was changed to Sunday, according to the Pope's declaration and NOT the Bible. This in effect makes the Church's authority above the Bible.

160 http://thewaybiblicalfellowship.com, accessed September 12, 2017.

Deception #2. The Sabbath - The Word of God that teaches us to observe the seventh day. The Sabbath has been replaced with a pagan day of worship, Sunday.

Deception #3. Arrangement of the Bible - The order of the Bible was changed to meet man's desire over the historically accepted order for God's Word.

As we journey through the End Times and its deception, keep in mind that language and culture are closely related. The words and expressions of a language may be "viewed as a verbal expression of culture. It is used to maintain and convey culture and cultural ties."[161]

From childhood to the present day, the values, traditions and customs of our Western World have shaped the way in which we think and understand the teachings of the Bible. A living language, such as English, moves and develops with each generation. Older languages like Hebrew and Aramaic are more static.

As previously established, when a person learns a second or third language, the learner is introduced to the culture of the language studied. Therefore, "culture has a crucial role in encoding and decoding messages" and supports the idea that "culture is at the heart of communication." In fact, it is the "body of knowledge of common

---

161 http://www.lexiophiles.com/uncategorized/the-relationship-between-language-and-culture, accessed September 12, 2017.

beliefs, behaviors and values appear to be the factor to establish and interpret meaning in both verbal and nonverbal language."[162]

As we have covered worldview and biblical thinking verses Greek thinking, there is one more area in which we may have been deceived. This deception is our arrogance. Granted, we who live in the West do not hold a patent on cultural bias. Most every ungodly, pagan society feels their perspective and cultural value are fine just like they are.

You may be thinking, so, how does this qualify as an *End Time Deception*? Well, we can raise the American flag right alongside the Christian flag. We can Pledge allegiance to God and country. We can place hard covered Bibles in our hotels and motels. We can wear necklaces with a cross attached. We can say to one another, "God bless you" when one sneezes. We can declare that our Founding Fathers were God-fearing men. *We can say anything.* Yet, there has never been a long running, God-fearing society in all of history. Even Israel did not continuously serve God faithfully. So, what is the point being made here? Unless we are fully obedient to God's Word, we are in sin. That is to say, unless we as a nation repent for our sins, then judgement is coming. John Piper puts it this way.

> So God taught his people not to say, "It is because of my righteousness that the LORD has brought me in to

---

162 Byram and Risager, *The Role of English language culture in the Omani language education system: An Ideological Perspective. Language, Culture and Curriculum*, 18 (3) 258-270. (1999, originally cited in Al-Issa, 2005 and in *Journal of Language Teaching and Research*, Vol. 4, No. 5, pp. 953-957, September 2013, http://www.academypublication.com/issues/past/jltr/vol04/05/07.pdf, accessed September 12, 2017.

possess this land." Rather, "it is because of the wickedness of these nations that the LORD is driving them out before you" (Deuteronomy 9:4).

...numerous texts in the Bible mention the kinds of iniquity God has in mind when he says, "the wickedness of these nations." Judgment to Israel and other nations is threatened for arrogant hearts (Isaiah 2:11; 3:15; 13:11), idolatry (Jeremiah 16:18; Ezekiel 23:20), bribery (Isaiah 1:23), extortion (Ezekiel 22:12), and the oppression of the poor (Isaiah 10:2; Malachi 3:4).

But there is a remarkable sequence of sins in Leviticus 18:20–25 that sounds very much like the progress of iniquity in the modern Western world. Moses writes that by these iniquities "the nations, which I am driving out before you, have become unclean, and the land became unclean, so that I punished its iniquity, and the land vomited out its inhabitants" (verse 25).

What brought the nations of Canaan to that point of judgment? Here are the sins Moses was referring to:

1. Adultery. Verse 20: "You shall not lie sexually with your neighbor's wife . . ."

2. Child sacrifice (we call it abortion). Verse 21: "You shall not give any of your children to offer them to Molech, and so profane the name of your God: I am the LORD."

3. Homosexual intercourse. Verse 22: "You shall not lie with a male as with a woman; it is an abomination."

4. Bestiality. Verse 23: "And you shall not lie with any animal and so make yourself unclean with it: . . . it is perversion."

In the West, we have moved to the point of open approval of adultery, child-killing, and homosexual intercourse. Will the open approval of bestiality be next? Probably. Last week, the Huffington Post reported a woman finding on her boyfriend's phone pictures of him having sex with her dog.[163]

My concern with the sins mentioned by Piper is that they occur within our society at large AND in our local churches!

Jeremiah 18:7-10
7 At one moment I may declare concerning a nation or a
kingdom, that I will pluck up and break down and destroy it, 8
but if that nation, concerning which I have spoken, turns from
its evil, I will change my mind about the disaster that I intended
to bring on it. 9 And at another moment I may declare
concerning a nation or a kingdom that I will build and plant it,
10 but if it does evil in my sight, not listening to my voice, then
I will change my mind about the good that I had intended to do
to it. (NRSV)

In Jeremiah 18 God tells us that if a nation does evil and does not repent, they are in danger of His judgment.

As of 2017, public support for legal abortion remains as high as it has been in two decades of polling. Currently, 57% say abortion should be legal in all or

163 Article by John Piper, http://www.desiringgod.org/articles/will-america-be-judged, accessed October 4, 2017.

> most cases, while 40% say it should be illegal in all or most cases.
>
> Though abortion is a divisive issue, more than half of U.S. adults take a non-absolutist position, saying that in most – but not all – cases, abortion should be legal (33%) or illegal (24%). Fewer take the position that in all cases abortion should be either legal (25%) or illegal (16%).[164]

These statics do not present us with any new information. Once more, what is my point? Sin is defined by only one source of authority. That source is the whole Bible. The Bible is not a list where you pick which items you desire and leave the rest. Obedience to the imperatives of the Bible is, or should be, a by-product of a Christ-centered life. Biblical truth should not be swayed by one's political or denominational affiliation.

The issues that we do not talk about, the hatred that we have buried in our hearts, the areas of the Internet that we browse in hopes that no one sees what we were doing, the thoughts we have about our neighbor, are most likely unconfessed sins.

Allow me to take one example from Genesis 4:10 to give greater clarity about abortion. And the LORD said, "What have you done? The voice of your brother's blood is crying to me from the ground" (ESV). The "blood" mentioned here literally means bloods. "The word is in the plural," implying that Cain's murder was not limited to his brother Abel. When Cain killed his brother, he also killed

164 http://www.pewforum.org/fact-sheet/public-opinion-on-abortion, accessed October 4, 2017.

all of "his potential descendants." In God's eyes, Cain killed them all. [165] In essence, Cain killed not one person but thousands.

The organization, National Right to Life, estimates that, "since the U.S. Supreme Court legalized abortion 43 years ago in Roe v. Wade and Doe v. Bolton, more than 58 million unborn children have lost their lives."[166] Not only is the blood of 58 million aborted children crying out to God, but the blood of billions that were murdered (their potential descendants). This is not a matter that Spirit-filled believers can causally ignore.

This deception is summed up in the words of Richard Wurmbrand: "I have suffered *more* from the *complacency of the West than from the Communist.*"(italics added)[167]

> Luke 18:9 (Parable of the Pharisee and the Tax Collector)
> He also told this parable to some who trusted in themselves that they were righteous and regarded others with contempt: (NRSV)

---

165 Scherman, Rabbi Nosson, and Rabbi Meir Zlotowitz, *The Chumash*. (Brooklyn, NY: Mesorah Publications, Ltd., 2000), 21.

166 http://www.lifenews.com/2016/01/14/58586256-abortions-in-america-since-roe-v-wade-in-1973, accessed October 4, 2017.

167 "The Voice of the Martyrs," October, 2017, 2. Note: Pastor Richard Wurmbrand (March 24, 1909 – February 17, 2001) was a Romanian evangelical minister and a Jew who spent fourteen years in Communist imprisonment and torture in his homeland of Romania. He was one of Romania's most widely known Jewish Believer leaders, authors, and educators. In 1945, when the Communists seized Romania and attempted to control the churches for their purposes, Richard Wurmbrand immediately began an effective "underground" ministry to his enslaved people and the invading Russian soldiers. He was eventually arrested in 1948. Richard spent three years in solitary confinement, seeing no one but his Communist torturers. (Source: http://richardwurmbrandbio.info, accessed October 5, 2017.

Deception #4 - My hands are clean as I stand before the LORD

CHAPTER NINE

Deception #5

Adopting an historical anti-Semitic & anti-Judaist attitude

Civilization was already in place when, in approximately 1800 B.C.E. – when the now-6,000-year-old recorded history of humankind had already passed its one-third mark – a man named Abraham entered the world stage.

Abraham declared that the sole Creator and Ruler of the universe is יהוה YHWH, the Lord God. (The actual pronunciation of the proper name of God has been lost for millennia. Today YHWH is pronounced אֲדֹנָי Adonai, literally, "our Master," the recognized and accepted substitute pronunciation.[168]

The tetragrammaton (tet·ra·gram·ma·ton) means consisting of four letters, יהוה is the biblical name of God. *Tetra* means four and *Grammat* means letter.[169]

---

168 Rabbi Wayne Dosick, *Living Judaism* (Harper Collins: San Francisco, CA, 1995), 4, 5.

169 In *Torah* God is acknowledged as Creator, Redeemer, Law-Giver, and Ruler. God is called by three proper names: *Elohim, Eyl*, and *Shaddai*. Later in the Bible God is called by names that reflect His nature and His role in His people. The name *Shechinah*, The Presence, is used to reflect God's all-enveloping presence. (Source: Dosick, *Living Judaism*, 8, 9.

The four Hebrew letters found in the biblical name of God:

י is the *Yod*
ה is the *He*
ו is the *Waw*
ה is the *He*

יהוה is Hebrew and the letters YHWH [yeh-ho-vaw'] are the Latin script. יהוה is the four-letter Biblical name of the God of Israel. YHWH is the God of Israel! Let this biblical fact settle into your heart. No other ethnic group can make claim to this one simple truth. God called Abraham, then his son Isaac, and then his grandson Jacob. Jacob's name was changed to Israel. Without any question, Scripture supports no other people, than Israel, as His chosen people.

Gregory IX became Pope in AD 1227. In AD 1231 he started the ball rolling in what became known as the Inquisition. The Inquisition was initially focused on Christian heretics; individuals that did not agree with the doctrine of the Catholic Church. These heretics were often tortured to bring about confession and conformity. Others were "handed over to secular authority to be burned at the stake – or, if they were lucky" had "their tongues removed." This sounds like the re-education camps in North Korea today!

The introduction "of logic as a missionary tool was a welcome relief to [Gentile] Christians because … arguing against Jews from their own Scriptures was such an abysmal failure."[170] As the use of human logic gained greater use in the Catholic Church's attempt to convert Jews, unknown at first, like using the Bible, failure was the end result.

170 Carroll, *Constantine's Sword*, 303

Thomas Aquinas thought that if he approached the Jews with the truth about Jesus, his human logic would win the day with mass conversions. The opposite occurred. His judgmental and arrogant response was that the Jews knew that "Jesus was the Messiah" and "murdered Him anyway."[171]

The problem was not a Jewish problem. In spite of grand plans and never ending attempts, Jews would not deny their God. Yes, there were forced baptisms and some Jews converted in the face of ongoing persecution, but a large scale conversion never occurred.

The history books are full of the full-scale attack against God's chosen people throughout Western Europe. This onslaught spanned hundreds of years. It led to ghettos long before Adolf Hitler's time.

A sad byproduct of the attacks against the Jews is that thousands upon thousands of Hebrew documents were systematically destroyed; the original Hebrew documents written by the Apostles among them. In AD 1242 there were "up to twenty-four cartloads of books" [172] publically burned in Paris.

> The first known ordered destruction of Jewish "books," recorded in 1 Maccabees 1:56, dates to the second century B.C.E., when the Syrian King sought to stamp out Jewish religion. "Any books of the Law they came to light were torn up and burned. Whenever anyone was discovered possessing a copy of the covenant or practicing the Law, the king's decrees sentenced him to death." The Nazis targeted Jewish books almost as ruthlessly as they did Jews. Assessing the destruction of nearly five-hundred

---

171 Ibid, 306

172 Ibid, 309

> mainly Jewish libraries in Nazi-controlled Europe, one historian concluded that five million or more Jewish books were destroyed. This does not include books in the households of 6 million Jews who were murdered.[173]

The challenge for us today - we have believed what we were taught through the Western theological lens. It was the Western religious leaders and theologians that gave birth to the Crusades that wrote the doctrine that we believe today. Be it Constantine's viewpoint or that of King James, their ungodly attitude poisoned the Western Church. This anti-Semitic view of these Gentile Church leaders determined that *if there was a problem, the Jews were guilty of causing it.* Even the Black Plague was blamed on the Jews.

In Spain, Ferdinand and Isabella married and thus united their kingdoms. The Spanish Inquisition began in 1492 and the "Jews had three months either to convert or get out of Spain."[174] During the Reformation, it was understood that the "Church's shaken faith"[175] was the fault of the Jews.

Martin Luther said that "next to the devil you have no enemy more cruel, more venomous and virulent, than a true Jew."[176]

Deception #5 - Adopting an historical anti-Semitic, anti-Judaist attitude

---

173 Ibid, 662
174 Ibid, 361
175 Ibid, 365
176 Carroll, *Constantine's Sword*, 368

CHAPTER TEN

Deception #6

All of Israel rejected God and His Son, the Messiah

> ... the Church of Christ acknowledges that, according to God's saving design, the beginnings of her faith and her election are found already among the Patriarchs, Moses and the prophets. She professes that all who believe in Christ-Abraham's sons according to faith (Gal. 3:7)-are included in the same Patriarch's call, and likewise that the salvation of the Church is mysteriously foreshadowed by the chosen people's exodus from the land of bondage. The Church, therefore, cannot forget that she received the revelation of the Old Testament through the people with whom God in His inexpressible mercy concluded the Ancient Covenant. Nor can she forget that she draws sustenance from the root of that well-cultivated olive tree onto which have been grafted the wild shoots, the Gentiles.(Rom. 11:17-24) Indeed, the Church believes that by His cross Christ, Our Peace, reconciled Jews and Gentiles. making both one in Himself. (Eph. 2:14-16)[177]

This has not been an exhaustive study of *End Time Deception.* For the most part, I focused on the authority of the organized,

177 *Nostra Aetate*, Pope Paul VI, October 28, 1965, http://www.vatican.va/archive/hist_councils/ii_vatican_council/documents/vat-ii_decl_19651028_nostra-aetate_en.html, accessed October 11, 2017.

institutional church, along with human authority, and how these two have usurped the authority of God and the authority of His Word found in the Bible.

The word, usurp means "to seize and hold (office, place, functions, powers, etc.) in possession by force or without right; to seize or exercise authority or possession wrongfully."[178]

As we look at *Deception #6*, the question before us is this: Is Jesus the Messiah more faithful than God the Father? Go to your Bible to the passage about the Abrahamic Covenant (Genesis 12).

It is my opinion that all discussions about salvation cannot be biblically or historically understood until one has digested the first book of *Torah* (Genesis 1:1 - 3:15; Genesis 12:1-3).

> Genesis 12:1-3
>
> Now the LORD said to Abram, "Go from your country [land] and your kindred and your father's house to the land that I will show you. (2) And I will make of you a great nation, and I will bless you and make your name great, so that you will be a blessing. (3) I will bless those who bless you, and him who dishonors you I will curse, and in you all the families of the earth shall be blessed." (ESV)

The covenant established in Genesis 12 is a single covenant that covers all people of all time. The entire world's population is separated into two distinct groups. One group includes all of the descendants of

178 https://www.merriam-webster.com/dictionary/usurp, accessed August 17, 2017

Abraham, Isaac, and Jacob (whose name was changed to Israel, Genesis 35:10). The second group are the nations; the non-Jewish peoples.

Back to our question: Is Jesus the Messiah more faithful than His Father? If we take Malachi 3:6 to be Truth, "For I the LORD do not change…", then this creates a problem for those who declare that all of Israel rejected the Messiah.

In Genesis 1:1-3 we have God the Father (*Elohim*), the Spirit of God (*Rauch Elohim*), and the Word of God (and God said…) which, of course, is the Messiah (John 1:14, "the Word became flesh…"). *Elohim*, God is not singular as an individual person is singular. *Elohim* does not mean gods as with false gods, which are many. *Elohim* is the plural of *El*, i.e., *El Olam* (the Everlasting God) and *El Shaddai* (the Almighty God). *Elohim* is the Father, the Spirit, and yes, the Son.

If God did not keep His promise to Jacob (Israel), then we Gentiles do not have hope, theologically speaking. Why? *God must not keep His Word.* But, we know that God does keep His Word and that He does not change. It is us humans that are constantly changing!

Historically speaking, a biblical covenant "was broken only when it became clear that the relationship was over. The end came when the relationship, not the rules, was broken" [179]

> Matthew 15:24
>
> But he answered and said to them, "I am not sent except to the sheep that have strayed from the house of Israel."[180]

---

179 E. Randolf Richards and Brandon J. O'Brien, *Misreading Scripture with Western Eyes* (Downers Grove: IVP Books, 2012), 166.

The Messiah came first for the "lost sheep of the house of Israel," (Matthew 15:24), basically the Israelites that had broken the relationship with God by serving pagan gods. Keep in mind that not all of Jacob's descendants broke the covenant with God, only some. After the lost sheep were reached, the Messiah then went to the nations, the Gentiles.

Israel is the "light for the nations" (Isaiah 42:6-7). The Savior of Israel is YHWH [yeh-ho-vaw']; the LORD (Isaiah 43:11). We non-Jewish believers are grafted into Israel. We are the "nations." I do not want to scramble your theological eggs without a purpose. The lost sheep had to be reached so that they could in turn reach the nations; the people of the bottom line of the Abrahamic Covenant.

> Daniel 7:25
>
> "He shall *speak words against the Most High*, **and** shall wear out *the saints of the Most High*, **and** shall think *to change the times and the law*; **and** they shall be given into **his** hand for a *time, times, and half a time*." (ESV, italics and bold added)

[180] *The Original Aramaic New Testament in Plain English with Psalms & Proverbs* (8th edition with notes). This is a translation (8th edition-2013) of The Aramaic New Testament (Aramaic was the language of Jesus and his countrymen of 1st century Israel) in an English prose translation of The Peshitta New Testament. A translation of the Psalms & Proverbs from the ancient Peshitta OT Version is included at the end. This translation is derived from the author's Aramaic-English Interlinear New Testament and The Psalms & Proverbs interlinear. Aramaic was used in Mel Gibson's film "The Passion of the Christ" to make the film as realistic and accurate as possible.

Did you notice the four separate, yet overlapping, effects of this prophecy?

1. "He (the Enemy of God) shall "speak words against the Most High,"
2. and "shall wear out the saints (Israel) of the Most High,"
3. and "shall think to change the times and the law;"
4. and they (Israel) "shall be given into his hand for a time, times, and half a time."

"Speak words against the Most High, and shall wear out *the saints of the Most High"* (Daniel 7:25). The second part of this passage, which can be quantitatively and objectively measured over the past 2,500 years, is what the Enemy has done to God's saints, in particular; Israel. The Enemy has used us Gentile believers to fulfill the prophetic words of Daniel 7:25!

It has not been my desire to attack or judge the Catholic Church. I am just sharing the historical evidence that still influences us today. Every Protestant Church is, in a way, a daughter of the Roman Catholic Church. Protestants broke from the Catholic Church; therefore it is almost impossible to remove the influences that were imbedded over hundreds of years. We, the Protestant Church, still retain many of the values and theologies of the Catholic Church.

Adolf Hitler and his followers justified their atrocities to the Jewish people by the writings of Martin Luther, in particular, Luther's book, *On the Jews and Their Lies*. Martin Luther was one of the 16th century Protestant Reformers. We have all been influenced by Martin Luther.

During the early 20th Century, the Pope excommunicated Communist members of the Catholic Church. In Hitler's opinion, "Christianity was a religion fit only for slaves."[181] Yet, he remained a member of the Catholic Church for his whole life. To the Jews that experienced the atrocities of the Third Reich, Adolf Hitler was a "Christian." Even after so many years, it is no wonder Jews today do not trust the Christian community. In their view, some may feel that on some level we are like Hitler in our attitude towards them.

It was not until the 1960s that the Catholic Church faced the reality that Jesus and His disciples were all Jews! Keep in mind that the Enemy of God always seeks to disrupt God's plan.[182] Apparently, the descendants of Jacob (Israel) are a key part of God's present and future plans, if not; the Enemy would not continue to try to eliminate them. The Enemy has used the Church on numerous occasions in an effort to eliminate the Jewish population. Unless you have studied this, you may not know the facts. Here are a few from the historical account:

- **AD 66-70**, the First Jewish–Roman War ended with destruction of the Second Temple and the fall of

181 Bullock, Alan, *Hitler: A Study in Tyranny*. (New York: HarperCollins, 1991), 218.

182 **1 Peter 5:8**, "Be sober-minded; be watchful. Your adversary the devil prowls around like a roaring lion, seeking someone to devour."(ESV).
Matthew 16:23, But he turned and said to Peter, "Get behind me, Satan! You are a hindrance to me. For you are not setting your mind on the things of God, but on the things of man."(ESV).
2 Corinthians 11:14, "And no wonder, for even Satan disguises himself as an angel of light." (ESV)

Jerusalem. 1,100,000 Jews are killed by the Romans during the siege, and 100,000 captured and enslaved.[183]

- **AD 131–136.** Simon bar Kokhba (Bar Kosiba) leads a large Jewish revolt against Rome in response to Hadrian's actions. In the aftermath, the mostly Jewish population is annihilated (about 600,000 Jews killed) and Hadrian renames the province of Judea to *Syria Palaestina*, and attempts to root out Judaism.[184]
- **AD 1066.** Muslim mob stormed the royal palace in Granada, crucified Jewish vizier Joseph ibn Naghrela and massacred most of the Jewish population of the city. "More than 1,500 Jewish families, numbering 4,000 persons, fell in one day."[185]
- **AD 1095–1291**. Under the authority of the Church, Christian Crusades killed tens of thousands of Jews throughout Europe and in the Middle East.
- **AD 1516.** Ghetto of Venice is established as the first Jewish ghetto in Europe. Many others would follow.

---

183 Koninklijke Brill NV Leiden, *The Jewish Revolt Against Rome: Interdisciplinary Perspectives,* (IDC Publishers, The Netherlands, 2011), 224.

184 Jeffrey M. Shaw, Timothy J. Demy, *War and Religion: An Encyclopedia of Faith and Conflict* (ABC-CLIO: Santa Barbara, CA, 2017), 114-115.

185 Richard Gottheil, Meyer Kayserling, Granada, http://jewishencyclopedia.com/articles/6855-granada, accessed October 11, 2017.

- **1881–1884, 1903–1906, 1918–1920.** Three major waves of pogroms[186] kill tens of thousands of Jews in Russia and Ukraine.
- **1882–1903.** The First *Aliyah*[187] - a major wave of Jewish immigrants to build a homeland in biblical Israel.
- **1917.** The British defeat the Turks and gain control of Palestine. The British issue the *Balfour Declaration.* This provides official British support for "the establishment in Palestine of a national home for the Jewish people ... it being clearly understood that nothing shall be done which may prejudice the civil and religious rights of existing non-Jewish communities in Palestine". Many Jews interpret this to mean that all of Palestine was to become a Jewish state.[188]
- **1917.** The Russian civil war leads to over 2,000 pogroms with tens of thousands murdered and hundreds of thousand made homeless.

---

186 A pogrom is a word used to designate an attack, accompanied by destruction, looting of property, murder, and rape, perpetrated by one section of the population against another.
(Source: http://www.jewishvirtuallibrary.org/pogroms, accessed October 28, 2017.)

187 The term *aliyah*, going up to Israel, is used in Genesis in reference to our forefather Jacob's bones being brought from Egypt to what would be the Land of Israel: "And Joseph returned to Egypt, he and his brothers, and all who had gone up with him to bury his father, after he had buried his father." The Hebrew word *aliyah* translates as "elevation" or "going up." It is, in fact, used both for being called up to the Torah reading and for moving to the Land of Israel. http://www.chabad.org/library/article_cdo/aid/1584066/jewish/What-Does-Aliyah-Mean.htm, accessed October 19, 2017.

188 *Balfour Declaration*, http://www.jewishvirtuallibrary.org/text-of-the-balfour-declaration, accessed October 11, 2017.

- **1919.** February 15: Over 1,200 Jews killed in Khmelnitsky pogrom. March 25: Around 4,000 Jews killed by Cossack[189] troops in Tetiev. June 17: 800 Jews decapitated in assembly-line fashion in Dubovo.[190]
- **1938-1945.** The Holocaust (*Ha Shoah*), resulted in the methodical extermination of nearly 6 million Jews across Europe.

In case you did not know, "holocaust"[191] as used to reference the genocide of Hitler during WWII is from a Greek word meaning "burnt offering." It is as if the non-Jews had made a "burnt offering" to God of the Jews through the atrocities during the holocaust.

Jews refer to the holocaust as *Shoah*, which means "catastrophe."[192]

In a photo showing the entry to the concentration camp Auschwitz-Birkenau, Poland, in February/March 1945 reveals a

---

189 The term Cossack may include Ukrainians, Russians, Belarusians, Polish, Slovaks, or Hungarians.

190 https://www.haaretz.com/jewish/this-day-in-jewish-history/.premium-1.703233, accessed October 11, 2017.

191 "The Holocaust … is defined as the sum total of all anti-Jewish actions carried out by the Nazi regime between 1933 and 1945: from stripping the German Jews of their legal and economic status in the 1930s`; segregating and starvation in the various occupied countries; the murder of close to six million Jews in Europe. The Holocaust is part of a broader aggregate of acts of oppression and murder of various ethnic and political groups in Europe by the Nazis. Nevertheless, it has special significance due to the exceptional attitude with which its perpetrators – the Nazis – regarded their Jewish victims. In the Nazi terminology the Jews were referred to as "world Jewry," a term unparalleled with respect to any other ethnic, ideological, or social group. The Nazis' proclaimed goal was the eradication of European Jewry." (Source: http://www.yadvashem.org/yv/en/holocaust/resource_center/the_holocaust.asp, accessed August 31, 2017.

192 Carroll, *Constantine's Sword*, 11

Catholic Cross above the main entrance. As Avi Weiss, a senior rabbi of the Hebrew Institute of Riverdale and the author of the book *Open Up the Iron Door: Memoirs of a Soviet Jewry Activist,* states, "Auschwitz is a sacred place of Jewish memory. It's no place for a [cross of the] Catholic church."[193]

Elie Wiesel had it right when he stated, "What the Germans wanted to do to the Jewish people was to substitute themselves for the Jewish God."[194]

Susannah Heschel states, "the more Jewish Jesus could be shown to have been, the more Christians would respect Judaism."[195] However, for most of the past two-thousand years the opposite was true.

As it was on national news and the numerous videos on the Internet, most of us heard the neo-Nazis protesters in Charlottesville recently chanting against the Jews: "Jews will not replace us."[196]

If we were to ask these neo-Nazis marchers if they are Christians or if they are church members, would any say "Yes"?

1 John 3:10

By this it is evident who are the children of God, and who are the children of the devil: whoever does not practice

---

193 https://www.washingtonpost.com/posteverything/wp/2015/01/28, accessed January 1, 2018.

194 Elie Wiesel, "Talking and Writing and Keeping Silent," in F.H. Littell and H.G. Locke, *German Church Struggle,* (Detroit; Wayne State University Press, 1974), 274.

195 Susannah Heschel, *Abraham Geiger and the Jewish Jesus*, (The University of Chicago Press: Chicago, IL, 1998), 11.

196 August 12-13, 2017

righteousness is not of God, nor is the one who does not love his brother. (ESV)

If we take the epistle of 1 John, which echoes the Greatest Commandment to love our neighbors (Matthew 22:36-40; Mark 12:31), then to hate anyone, including Jews, then the protesters are potentially "children of the devil" (1 John 3:10).

We often overlook the fact that the early followers of the Messiah were Jews. The Twelve Apostles were Jews. In Acts 2:5, "Now there were staying in Jerusalem God-fearing Jews from every nation under heaven."[197] It was a city full of "God-fearing Jews" on the day of Pentecost.

> Acts 2:41
> "…and about three thousand [Jews] were added to their number that day." (NIV)

> Matthew 15:24
> "He answered, "I was sent only to the lost sheep of the house of Israel."[198] Jesus' first ministry was to the "lost sheep" of Israel and He was successful in reaching many of them. (ESV)

These "lost sheep" of Israel became the missionaries that carried the Good News to the nations and thereby fulfilled the bottom line of the Abrahamic Covenant.

---

197 NIV
198 ESV

Trivia: We are all familiar with the Parable of the Lost Sheep of Luke 15. Have you ever connected this parable with Matthew 15:24?

When the Messiah is presented in the biblical context, what I have found is that the Jews of today have not rejected the Messiah as pictured in the Bible. Rather, what they reject is us, the anti-Semitic, anti-Judaist, arrogant Western Christians with our ungodly, self-serving attitudes. They too reject the image of the Messiah that was birthed through the historic Catholic Church and that many today still propagate, such as the Church's attitude that supported the Crusades, forced baptism, Adolf Hitler, the KKK, neo-Nazis, etc.

When a non-Jewish believer expresses disregard or distain about the "Old Testament" and the "Law," what we are seeing is a heart tainted by racism and anti-Semitism. **There is a dark, demonic force behind those who close their ears to the truth about the relevance of the whole Bible today.**

A study of the history that covers the relationship between the institutional "Church" and the Jewish people proves that Daniel 7:25, by wearing "out the saints of the Most High" with an unrelenting desire to convert or kill them, has been fulfilled.

The Catholic Church is no more at fault than the Protestant Church when it comes to persecuting the Jewish people. With the influence of Martin Luther[199] and other Christian theologians, many view the Jews with suspicion.

199 AD 1483-1546

Luther declared that there was no "doubt that next to the devil you have no enemy more cruel, more venomous and virulent, then a true Jew."[200]

Luther's hatred is evident in the distinction between the Jews of ancient Israel and those in his day. He stated that "ancient Israelites, whom he boundlessly admired, and the Jews of the Christian era, whom he hated with increasing venom."[201]

At the beginning of his career, Martin Luther was apparently sympathetic to Jewish resistance to the Catholic Church. However, he expected the Jews to convert to his purified Christianity; when they did not, he turned violently against them.

Luther used violent and vulgar language throughout his career. While we do not expect religious figures to use this sort of language in the modern world, it was not uncommon [for them to do so] in the early 16th century.[202]

In an article titled, *Was Luther Anti-Semitic*? Written by Eric W. Gritsch, we read:

> "Set fire to their synagogues or schools," Martin Luther recommended in *On the Jews and Their Lies*. Jewish houses should "be razed and destroyed," and Jewish "prayer books and *Talmudic* writings, in which such idolatry, lies, cursing, and blasphemy are taught, [should] be taken from them." In addition, "their rabbis [should] be forbidden to teach on pain of loss of life and limb." Still, this wasn't enough.

200 Carroll, *Constantine's Sword*, 368

201 ibid

202 http://www.jewishvirtuallibrary.org/martin-luther-quot-the-jews-and-their-lies-quot, accessed September 5, 2017.

Luther also urged that "safe-conduct on the highways be abolished completely for the Jews," and that "all cash and treasure of silver and gold be taken from them." What Jews could do was to have "a flail, an ax, a hoe, a spade" put into their hands so "young, strong Jews and Jewesses" could "earn their bread in the sweat of their brow."

In 1523, Luther accused Catholics of being unfair to Jews and treating them "as if they were dogs," thus making it difficult for Jews to convert. "I would request and advise that one deal gently with them [the Jews]," he wrote. " … If we really want to help them, we must be guided in our dealings with them not by papal law but by the law of Christian love. We must receive them cordially, and permit them to trade and work with us, hear our Christian teaching, and witness our Christian life. If some of them should prove stiff-necked, what of it? After all, we ourselves are not all good Christians either."

Fifteen years later, however, rumors of Jewish efforts to convert Christians upset him, and he wrote a treatise venting his frustration. In it, Luther concluded that converting Jews had become hopeless.

It seemed to him that God had deserted the Jews, leaving them to wander homeless without a land or temple of their own. And if this was God's attitude, then one might with good conscience ignore the Jews. Why would God desert his own people if he did not despair of them? He had rejected them and turned his attention to the "new Israel," the Christian church. Luther thus accepted the existing notion that the promise given to Jews was now transferred to Christians.[203] (italics added)

203 http://www.christianitytoday.com/history/issues/issue-39/was-luther-anti-semitic.html, accessed September 5, 2017

Grasp Luther's hatred, as recorded in his 1543 pamphlet, [204] *Concerning the Jews and their Lies*, he "advocated the burning of synagogues" and the Jews should be "forbidden on the pain of death to praise God, to give thanks, to pray, and to teach publicly among us and in our country." [205] Luther was one of the primary leaders during the Reformation. His heart-felt attitude towards the Jews was carried through the years down to us today.

> Proverbs 10:12
> Hatred stirs up strife, but love covers all offenses. (ESV)

> Mark 12:29-31
> Jesus replied, "The most important commandment is this: 'Listen, O Israel! The LORD our God is the one and only LORD. And you shall love the Lord your God with all your heart and with all your soul and with all your mind and with all your strength.' The second is this: 'You shall love your neighbor as yourself.' There is no other commandment greater than these." (ESV)

To hate, as expressed by Martin Luther is contrary to the teaching of the Bible; it is wrong and non-biblical. When such an influential leader has a non-biblical hatred to another human being or ethnic group, this

---

[204] It was on October 31, 1517 that Martin Luther nailed 95 debate propositions on the door of the cathedral in Wittenberg. His views of the Jewish people were expressed twenty-six years later in the pamphlet, *Concerning the Jews and their Lies*.

[205] Carroll, *Constantine's Sword*, 367

"poison" spreads continually over time, all the way to Charlottesville, Virginia in 2017.

Background: The verses in Daniel 7 that lead up to verse 25: In verse 22 of Daniel 7, the expression, "Ancient of Days" is the title for God as Judge as found in prophetic passages in Daniel 7:9, 13, and 22. This title may also refer to the Messiah as Judge of the end-times events. The "Ancient of Days" judges all seven of the churches in Revelation 1–3.

> Revelation 2:4-5
>
> "But I have this against you, that you have abandoned the love you had at first. Remember therefore from where you have fallen; *repent*, and do the works you did at first. If not, *I will come to you and remove your lampstand* from its place, unless you repent." (ESV)

Lampstand is the menorah, the lamp of God. It takes a great deal of work to make a biblical menorah. The menorah is the Light of God in our congregations. If we do not do the will of God, He will remove His presence from the congregation.

> Revelation 2:11
>
> "He who has an ear, let him hear what the Spirit says to the churches. The *one who conquers will not be hurt by the second death*." (ESV)

This is not a passive life we are to live! We are to be "conquerors" of evil. Our lives should reflect absolute obedience to the Word; all of it. Revelation 2:16, "Therefore repent. If not, I will come to you soon and war against them with the sword of my mouth" (ESV). He will use a sword that brings about great grief for the congregation.

> Revelation 2:20
> "But I have this against you, that you tolerate that woman Jezebel, who calls herself a prophetess and is teaching and seducing my servants to practice sexual immorality and to eat food sacrificed to idols." (ESV)

Jezebel, through her "teaching and seducing," exercises control over the people. Therefore, Jezebel is a controlling person, or a controlling group of people, that the others in the congregation tolerate or ignore. This tolerance exist while Jezebel does the work of Satan in their midst.

> Revelation 3:2
> "Wake up, and strengthen what remains and is about to die, for I have not found your works complete in the sight of my God." (ESV)

The task the Lord has given them has not been accomplished.

Revelation 3:15-16

"I know your works: you are neither cold nor hot. Would that you were either cold or hot! So, because you are lukewarm, and neither hot nor cold, I will spit you out of my mouth." (ESV)

These "Christian" people make the Lord so sick that He will vomit them out of His mouth.

The Bible tells us that Antichrist will arise out of "the sea"[206] (Daniel 7:2-3, Revelation 13:1) indicating that he will arise out of the gentile nations, not Israel. Antichrist will be the *blasphemous horn* (blasphemous horn means power that works against the LORD) of Daniel 7:24-25. As told in Second Thessalonians 2:3, due to the great falling away, many people will follow the antichrist (Revelation 13:3).

Daniel tells us that "there shall be a time of trouble, such as never was since there was a nation even to that same time" (Daniel 12:1). This "time of trouble" is upon us. Although there will be greater anti-Semitism and anti-Judaism, this time of trouble will contain something never seen before. That is to say, throughout history people have worshiped false gods and they will continue to do so. Yet, there

---

206 "To say that the Antichrist is to be a Jew would contradict the very nature of the times of the Gentiles. . . two different beasts are described as arising from the 'sea' and the 'earth.' The 'sea' is a literary image that often indicates the 'Gentile nations'" (source: https://www.biblestudytools.com/ commentaries/revelation/ related-topics/jewish-or-gentile.html, accessed March 7, 2018).

"The Bible makes it clear that he will be a Gentile. In Revelation 13:1 he is portrayed as a "beast coming up out of the sea." The sea is used consistently throughout the prophetic scriptures as a symbol of the Gentile nations (Daniel 7:3; Luke 21:25; and Revelation 17:1)." (source: http://christinprophecy.org/articles/the-rise-and-fall-of-the-antichrist, accessed March 7, 2018.

will be such a false "Christianity" that, because of the degree of deception, many of those involved are completely deceived.

He shall speak words against the Most High. The "He" refers to the Enemy of God that will take actions against *Elyon* (the Most High God) as the ultimate authority. *Ha satan* (who we call Satan) wants to be worshiped! This Enemy of God shall redefine what biblical "truth" is. As we have seen, it has already begun! *The saints of the Most High* are the true Israel, which we Gentile believers are grafted into.

In Romans 11 there are two key points Paul wants us to understand. First, God has not rejected Israel; and second, the olive tree is Israel's present reminder of their future national salvation in Yeshua. In Scripture, "Israel is pictured" as "a garden of God:"[207]

1. The Fig tree, biblically symbolized Israel's national life, (Hosea 9:10; Mark. 11:12-14, 20; Matthew. 24:32-34).
2. The Vine, biblically symbolized Israel's spiritual life, (Isaiah 5:1-7; Psalm 80:9; Hosea 10:1, John 15:1-6).
3. The Olive tree, biblically symbolized Israel's ministerial or service life, (Jeremiah 11:16, Hosea 14:6; Romans 11:16-24).

In Romans 11:17 it is critical to understand that only "some of the branches were broken off." People may say that God is now through with Israel as a national witness, however Paul says it is only the unbelieving natural branches, as many as they may be, that are broken off from Israel. Unbelief and disobedience brings loss of service.

---

207 Sam Nadler, http://www.messianicassociation.org/ezine17-sn.olive.htm, accessed October 11, 2017.

In fact, Israel as a witness nation was both then and is "at this present time" continuing on through the believing natural branches, and including the testimony of the grafted-in wild branches; Gentiles such as Ruth and Rahab (see Joshua 2, Hebrews 11:31)! If you're a Gentile believer, "you too have been grafted in among them, not to replace Jews, but among the Jewish people … Jewish believers are not grafted into a Gentile Church. Quite the opposite: Paul says that Gentile believers, as wild olive branches, are grafted into a Jewish tree!"[208]

(See Appendix D for the story about Zacchaeus like you may not have read it before.)

T*o change the times and the law* means the Enemy of God will change the appointed time periods or epochs of time ***and*** to change the Word, the law, the decrees of God. The Bible says that the saints, God's chosen people, *shall be given into his hand for a time, times, and half a time*. This prophecy was given in 552 BC and was fulfilled 2,500 years later in AD 1948.

> Isaiah 66:8
> "Who has heard such a thing? Who has seen such things? Shall a land be born in one day? Shall a nation be brought forth in one moment? For as soon as Zion was in labor she brought forth her children."(ESV)

This Scripture was fulfilled 70 years ago!

208 Sam Nadler, http://www.messianicassociation.org/ezine17-sn.olive.htm, accessed August 18, 2017

> Matthew 24:32-34
>
> "From the fig tree learn its lesson: as soon as its branch becomes tender and puts out its leaves, you know that summer is near. So also, when you see all these things, you know that he is near, at the very gates. I tell you the truth; this generation will not pass from the scene until all these things take place." (ESV)

Matthew 24:32-34 speaks of the blooming fig tree and how that generation will not die before the end occurs.

> Trivia: Many scholars and historians date Jesus' crucifixion to either Friday, April 7, AD 30 or Friday, April 3, AD 33. Matthew, Mark, and Luke each record that Jesus died about "the ninth hour".[209] Therefore, if we conclude that the end of the second epoch (the period of *Torah*) ended with Jesus saying "…'*It is finished*,' and he bowed his head and gave up his spirit" in John 19:30 (ESV, italics added), then, if one of these dates in April marks the end of the second 2,000 year epoch (the period of the *Torah*), and not to the actual date the Herodian temple was destroyed (AD 70), then this third and last 2,000 year epoch (days of the Messiah) will end in the year of 2030 or 2033 (12-15 years from today in 2018).

---

209 Matthew 27:45-50, Mark 15:34-37, Luke 23:44-46

Israel became a nation once again in 1948 after being dispersed around the world for almost 2,000 years.[210]

> Matthew 24:24
>
> "For *false Christs and false prophets* will arise and perform great signs and wonders, so as to lead astray, if possible, even the *elect.*"(ESV, italics added)

False Christs and false prophets are leaders that are really out to deceive. They will present false interpretations of the Bible and false avenues of salvation, even though the outward manifestations and religious activities seem the same. The "elect" cannot be deceived by this false presentation of "false truth" that is not from God.

The following Scriptures express God's special relationship with Israel.

> Isaiah 45:15, 17, 25
>
> (15) Truly, O God of Israel, our Savior, you work in *mysterious ways.*
>
> (17) But *Israel is saved by the LORD with everlasting salvation*; you shall not be put to shame or confounded to all eternity.
>
> (25) *In the LORD all the offspring of Israel shall be justified and shall glory.*" (ESV, italics added)

---

210 Israel became a nation at midnight May 14th, 1948. Israel becoming a nation fulfilled such prophecies as Ezekiel 36 and 37 and signaled the soon end of the age (of the Messiah). During the Six Day War, June 5-10, 1967, the temple mount was captured along with east Jerusalem by Israel.

Isaiah 51:16

And I have put my words in your mouth and covered you in the shadow of my hand, establishing the heavens and laying the foundations of the earth, and saying to Zion, "*You are my people*." (ESV, italics added)

Isaiah 54:5, 7

(5) For *your Maker is your husband*, the LORD of hosts is his name; and the Holy One of Israel is your *Redeemer*, the God of the whole earth he is called. (7) For a brief moment I deserted you, but with great compassion I will gather you. (ESV, italics added)

> Here is a clear statement in the Bible of the relationship between Yeshua's first and second comings. His first coming fulfilled the prophecy of Isaiah 52:13 – 53:12, which predicted that the Messiah would die as an atonement for human sin and be raised from the dead, so that he could **appear a second time** to fulfill such prophecies as Isaiah 2:2 – 5 and 9:5 – (6-7), which say that the Messiah will bring peace to the world and deliver his people Israel from oppression. However, since "not everyone from Israel is truly part of Israel" (Ro. 9:6), only **those who are eagerly waiting for** Yeshua's return can have assurance that they will be delivered.[211]

If you read only commentaries written by Western theologians you may not have an accurate commentary on these passages. Isaiah is

211 David Stern, *Jewish New Testament Commentary,* (Jewish New Testament Publications, Inc.: Clarksville, MD, 1996), 702.

addressing Israel, Jacob's descendants. Isaiah is NOT speaking of the Gentiles (the nations) that are later saved through the Messiah.

This passage speaks both to the captivity during the Babylonian time period, but also to the future when the Jewish people suffer death and isolation under the Western, institutional "Church." This "brief moment", for the most part, ended when Israel became a nation in 1948. Although anti-Semitism still exists, Jews have a homeland they can now go to.

> Isaiah 65:8-9
> Thus says the LORD: "As the new wine is found in the cluster, and they say, 'Do not destroy it, for there is a blessing in it,' so I will do for my servants' sake, and *not destroy them all.* I will bring forth *offspring from Jacob, and from Judah* possessors of my mountains; *my chosen* shall possess it, and *my servants* shall dwell there. (ESV, italics added)

From these passages, and many more can be added, we see that God has a special relationship with Israel. Try as we may to fully understand this relationship, it is a mystery to us.

> Acts 13:44-49
> 44 The next Sabbath almost the whole city gathered to hear the word of the Lord. 45 But when the Jews [refers here to non-believing Jewish religious leaders] saw the crowds [of Jewish people], they were filled with jealousy and began to contradict

> what was spoken by Paul, reviling him. 46 And Paul and Barnabas spoke out boldly, saying, "It was necessary that the word of God be spoken first to you [those who had been influenced by non-believing leaders]. Since you thrust it aside and judge yourselves unworthy of eternal life, behold, we are turning to the Gentiles [non-Jews]. 47 For so the Lord has commanded us, saying, "'I have made you [Israel] a light for the Gentiles, that you [Israel] may bring salvation to the ends of the earth.'" 48 And when the Gentiles heard this, they began rejoicing and glorifying the word of the Lord, and as many as were appointed to eternal life believed. 49 And the word of the Lord was spreading throughout the whole region. (ESV)

Verse 47 contains Isaiah 49:6: "It is too light a thing that you should be my servant to raise up the tribes of Jacob *and to bring back the preserved of Israel*; I will make you as *a light for the nations*, that my salvation may reach to the end of the earth"(ESV, italics added).

> Isaiah 49:6-7
>
> he says: "It is too light a thing that you should be my servant to raise up the tribes of Jacob and to bring back the preserved of Israel; *I will make you as a light for the nations, that my salvation may reach to the end of the earth.* Thus says *the LORD, the Redeemer of Israel* and his Holy One, to one deeply despised, abhorred by the nation, the servant of rulers: "Kings shall see and arise; princes, and they shall prostrate themselves; because of the

> LORD, who is faithful, the Holy One of Israel, *who has chosen you.*" (ESV, italics added)

Without Israel, the Gentile nations are without hope of salvation. We need Israel, they do not need us. That is to say, the Messiah came through Israel. Israel did not chose God, rather, God chose Israel. We Gentiles, once drawn to Christ by the Holy Spirit, choose redemption through the Messiah so that we may have a relationship with the Father.

Fact: Before the events of the first century, for the most part, we Gentiles were completely without hope of knowing God's saving grace. Israel was already God's chosen people and covered by the top line of the Abrahamic Covenant. We, the nations and people of the bottom line of the Covenant, needed a Messiah.

Unless God takes the initial step to reveal Himself to us, all men remain enslaved in the Kingdom of Darkness. John 3:27 (KJV), "… A man can receive nothing, except it be given him from heaven." Even though we may try, the need for a Savior cannot be conveyed from one human to another without the dynamism of the Holy Spirit – God must be directly involved. The greatest salesperson cannot, under any circumstance, led a sinner to Christ without the Holy Spirit (God) revealing Himself to the sinner. Yes, a salesperson may talk a sinner into saying a prayer, which only leads to false security.

John 6:44

"No man can come to me, except the Father which hath sent me draw him: and I will raise him up at the last day" [KJV, italics added].

Here is our only way to escape the clutches of *ha satan*; our freedom rests solely in the Father's Hands. The Father must "draw" us unto Himself. Believers, the laborers in God's vineyard, follow the Father's led as we "go and make disciples."

The sinner's calling unto salvation is when God reveals Himself to the non-believer for the purpose of saving the sinner's soul.

On the *Discipleship Continuum*, the *Seeker* is drawn by the Holy Spirit to the Father and to the Son. Once the calling from God begins to produce the fruit, then the seeds of faith from God become alive in the person; the calling of the Holy Spirit is experienced. [212]

Genesis 12:1-3

(Notice the "*I will*" statements made by the LORD)

Now the LORD said to Abram, "Go from your country [land] and your kindred and your father's house to the land that **I will** show you. (2) And **I will** make of you a great nation, and **I will** bless you and make your name great, so that you will be a blessing. (3) **I will** bless those who bless you, and him who

212 Michael Reilly, *The Journey from Darkness to Light* (Createspace Independent Publishing; Middletown, DE, 2017), 70-77.

dishonors you **I will** curse, and in you all the families of the earth shall be blessed." (ESV, bold added)

What role does Abraham have in this contract? (Be available! Be obedient!) That goes for all of Abraham, Isaac and Jacob's descendants. Disobedience to God's commandments, without repentance, would remove them from this covenant.

Jeremiah 4:1-2
"If you return, O Israel, declares the LORD, to me you should return. If you remove your detestable things from my presence, and do not waver, and if you swear, 'As the LORD lives,' in truth, in justice, and in righteousness, then nations shall bless themselves in him, and in him shall they glory."

Nehemiah 1:5
Then I said: "Lord, the God of heaven, the great and awesome God, who keeps his covenant of love with those who love him and keep his commandments (NIV).

Joel 2:31
And it shall come to pass that everyone who calls on the name of the LORD shall be saved. For in Mount Zion and in Jerusalem there shall be those who escape, as the LORD has said, and among the survivors shall be those whom the LORD calls. (ESV)

What ethic group was Abraham a part of? He was a direct descendant of Noah's son, Shem. There are ten generations from Noah to Abraham. Abraham was born in approximately 1,948 years after Adam. Ur of the Chaldees was the original home of Abraham. It was the capital of the ancient Chaldean Empire in ancient Mesopotamia.

In looking back at the covenant with Abraham, did you notice something at the end of Genesis 12 verse 3…"and all people;" nations, ethne will be blessed through Abraham, then Isaac, and Jacob

Around the year 1900 BC the Lord told Abraham to leave his home and country, and go to a land that He would show him. The last part of verse 3, "and in you all the families of the earth shall be blessed." This part of verse three can be seen as the "bottom line of the Abrahamic Covenant."

Until the Messiah was born, lived, died and was resurrected, in a real sense and with few exceptions, we Gentiles were without hope for salvation.

Salvation was reserved for God's chosen people; the descendants of Jacob (Israel). They were covered by the top line of the Abrahamic Covenant. This bottom line of the Abrahamic Covenant could be viewed as the part of the covenant that affects us Gentiles. We Gentile believers are blessed because of Abraham; the Jewish people. What a brilliant plan, a single covenant with "a twofold way to salvation."[213] "It is a tragedy of major proportions that we failed for so long to see that

213 Norbert Lohfink, *The Covenant Never Revoked: Biblical Reflections on Christian-Jewish Dialogue* (Paulist Press: Mahwah, NJ, 1991), 83.

this was the universal God's particular calling for us [Gentile believers], alongside Israel's particular calling."[214]

Isaiah 49:6, "…I will make you as a light for the nations, that my salvation may reach to the end of the earth." Abraham, Isaac and Jacob, and their descendants that continued to worship God are the elect. Deuteronomy 7:6-8 puts it this way,

> Deuteronomy 7:6-8
> "For you are a people holy to the LORD your God. The LORD your God has chosen you to be a people for his treasured possession, out of all the peoples who are on the face of the earth. It was not because you were more in number than any other people that the LORD set his love on you and chose you, for you were the fewest of all peoples, but it is because the LORD loves you and is keeping the oath that he swore to your fathers, that the LORD has brought you out with a mighty hand and redeemed you from the house of slavery, from the hand of Pharaoh king of Egypt." (ESV).

> Ephesians 2:12
> Remember that you were at that time separated from Christ, alienated from the commonwealth of Israel and strangers to the covenants of promise, having no hope and without God in the world. (ESV)

---

214 Eugene J. Fisher, *Visions of the Others* (Paulist Press: Mahwah, NJ, 1994), 65.

We Gentiles believers are grafted into Israel - we become Jews. Sadly, often when conversing about the state of Israel, we default to repeating what we have heard others say; which is at times colored by anti-Semitism. Seldom do we have this conversation based upon our own objective study of the Bible.

In Romans 11:26-27 we read, "Lest you be wise in your own sight, I do not want you to be unaware of this mystery, brothers [and sisters]: a *partial hardening has come upon Israel, until the fullness of the Gentiles has come in.* And in this way all Israel will be saved, as it is written 'The Deliverer will come from Zion, he will banish ungodliness from Jacob'; and this will be my covenant with them when *I take away their sins*" (italics added, ESV). (This passage pulls in Isaiah 59:20, 21; 27:9; Jeremiah 31:33, 34.)

What occurs between God and Israel is God's business. He has not asked us for our opinions. We should be as wise as Pope Paul VI when he declares that **the eternal covenant between God and the People of Israel has not been broken.** [215]

Even though the Jewish population makes up only about 0.02% of the world's population, they have been awarded 22 percent of Nobel Prizes. This is a profound fact. Yet, many Evangelic Christians will say that the Church has replaced Israel as God's chosen people. Are we so prideful or blind in our inherited theology that we do not question what we have been taught? Even a pagan can see that God's hand is upon Israel.

---

215 Pope Paul VI, in 1965 made this declaration *Nostra Aetate* to, in part; address the relationship between the Catholic Church and the Jewish people.

During the first century, in the city of Rome, one half of the population was enslaved.[216] Although there is some uncertainty as to how many Jews lived in or around Jerusalem in the first century, the "ration of Jewish dead…at the hands of the Romans" most likely was "one in three" persons. [217] Many of which were crucified. Think of this the next time you see a picture with three crosses on a hillside. The truth be known, there were probably hundreds of crosses, not only three.

The text we call the New Testament was written during a violent period of time for the Jewish people. The Temple was destroyed in AD 70 and what was left was burned in AD 135.

If we fail to grasp the hostile environment for the Jewish people during the first century, it would be like reading the book, *The Diary of Ann Frank* without any knowledge or reference to the Holocaust. (Between 1939 and 1945, six million were executed. These six million people were from at least 14 countries. Jews living outside of Germany were deported to one of the many concentration camps.)[218]

Who has really been deceived? According to the George Barna Group, over the past ten years, the number of adults who are unchurched has increased by more than 30%. This is an increase of 38 million people—that's about the population of Canada.

---

216 A. N. Wilson, *Paul, The Mind of an Apostle* (WW Norton & Company: New York, NY, 1997), 3

217 Carroll, *Constantine's Sword*, 303

218 Ibid, 90.

Today we have one-third fewer churches than we had in 1950. Of the total Protestant churches in the USA, 80% of the churches are either stagnant (without any growth) or they are about to close their doors.

Of all local churches in the USA, only 2 or 3% are growing because people are coming into a saving relationship with God the Father and His Son. From my assessment, we will live to see half of all local churches in the USA shut their doors within our lifetime. According to Christianity Today, there are "approximately 38,000" Christian denominations.[219]

In China there were "834 thousand evangelicals in 1949 when evangelism was freely permitted, but today nearly 100 million house-church believers exist under great persecution."[220] Around four to eight million Chinese come to know the Messiah every year!

Will it take persecution for American Christians to be awakened?

Matthew 24:24 tells us that the elect (the faithful Hebrews) cannot be deceived.

Jeremiah 31:35-37

Thus says *the LORD, who gives the sun for light by day and the fixed order of the moon and the stars for light by night*, who stirs up the sea so that its waves roar— the LORD of hosts is his name: "*If this*

---

219 http://blogforthelordjesuscurrentevents.com/2012/03/29/how-many-christian-denominations-are-there/, accessed July 13, 2017

220 Jerry Nelson, *Stepping Through Troubled Times*, (WestBow Press: Bloomington, IN, 2011), 83

> *fixed order departs from before me, declares the LORD, then shall the offspring of Israel cease from being a nation before me forever.*" Thus says the LORD: "If the heavens above can be measured, and the foundations of the earth below can be explored, then I will cast off all the offspring of Israel for all that they have done, declares the LORD." (ESV, Italics added)

Has the order of the sun, moon or stars changed or ceased to shine? No. Therefore, if God truly rejected Israel, then God has gone against His Word as stated in Jeremiah 31:35-37. Granted, many from the linage of Jacob have forsaken the LORD, much like us Gentiles (Hebrews 6:4-6).

If we take note of the wording in Jeremiah 31:31-33, we see a new covenant mentioned. "Behold, the days are coming, declares the LORD, when I will make *a new covenant with the house of Israel and the house of Judah*, not like the covenant that I made with their fathers on the day when I took them by the hand to bring them out of the land of Egypt, my covenant that they broke, though *I was their husband*, declares the LORD. For this is the covenant that I will make with the house of Israel after those days, declares the LORD: *I will put my law within them, and I will write it on their hearts.* And I will be their God, and they shall be my people. (ESV, Italics added)

With whom is God making this new covenant? (Israel and Judah[221]) Without God's chosen people (the descendants of Jacob), then we Gentiles cannot be grafted into something that does not exists. To make this out as a "spiritual grafting" is to view this with a Greek mindset. To graft a seedling into a dead tree serves no purpose as the seedling needs the life-giving roots of a living tree for the graft to live and grow (Romans 11:11-24). We need the wealth of wisdom and knowledge of the Hebrew Bible (our Old Testament) to fully understand the LORD's interaction with us in the past, with us today, and with us in the future. The bottom line of the Abrahamic Covenant is useless without the top line of the covenant.

> Romans 11:1-6
>
> I ask then: *Did God reject his people? By no means*! I am an Israelite myself, a descendant of Abraham, from the tribe of Benjamin. God did not reject his people, whom he foreknew. Don't you know what Scripture says in the passage about Elijah—how he appealed to God against Israel: "Lord, they have killed your prophets and torn down your altars; I am the only one left, and they are trying to kill me"? And what was God's answer to him? *"I have reserved for myself seven thousand who have not bowed the knee to Baal."* So too, at the present time there is a remnant chosen by

221 Israelites had a single kingdom during the reigns of Solomon and David. After the death of Solomon, the country was divided into two independent kingdoms. The southern region came to be called Judah which consisted of the tribes of Benjamin and Judah. Jerusalem was their capital. The northern region was called Israel which comprised the remaining ten tribes. They had the capital at Samaria. (www.differencebetween.net/miscellaneous/culture-miscellaneous/difference-between-israel-and-judah, accessed August 23, 2017)

grace. And if by grace, then it cannot be based on works; if it were, grace would no longer be grace. (ESV, Italics added)

Romans 11 makes it very clear that God did not reject Israel. It is truly a mystery for us, but Scriptures states in Romans 11:29 that "all Israel will be saved." Israel will once again possess the land promised to them (Deuteronomy 30:1–10). No such promise is made to the nations, the non-Jews.

The confusion sets in when we humans try to explain this "mystery" theologically. Sadly, some theologians speak as if they fully understand God's views on a host of biblical issues. They should be more like the German theologian, Nicolaus of Cusa, who viewed God, as "transcending total comprehension by human beings."[222] He argued that man could not fully know or understand God. We would be wise to take the same humble attitude.

I have already mentioned the expression *Nostra Aetate* (*no stra i-tate*, Latin for *In Our Time*). This was the beginning of a major shift in the Catholic Church's historic view and attitude towards the Jews. This was a major course correction on their part. In doing so, the Pope moved closer to a biblical attitude toward the Jews and Israel than most Protestants in the Western world.

Pope Paul VI, in 1965 made the declaration *Nostra Aetate* to, in part, address the relationship between the Catholic Church and the Jewish people. In this declaration, in Section 4, the Pope declares that **the eternal covenant between God and the People of Israel has**

222 Carroll, *Constantine's Sword*, 350

not been broken. He further states that the Catholic Church should not attempt to baptize (evangelize) Jews any longer. Unless you have studied the history of the persecution of the Jewish people by the Catholic Church then the full weight of this declaration is missed. Here is part of the Pope's declaration.

> As the sacred synod [assembly] searches into the mystery of the Church, it remembers the bond that spiritually ties the people of the New Covenant to Abraham's stock. Thus the Church of Christ acknowledges that, according to God's saving design, the beginnings of her faith and her election are found already among the Patriarchs, Moses and the prophets. She professes that all who believe in Christ-Abraham's sons according to faith (Gal. 3:7)-are included in the same Patriarch's call, and likewise that the salvation of the Church is mysteriously foreshadowed by the chosen people's exodus from the land of bondage. The Church, therefore, cannot forget that she received the revelation of the Old Testament through the people with whom God in His inexpressible mercy concluded the Ancient Covenant. Nor can she forget that she draws sustenance from the root of that well-cultivated olive tree onto which have been grafted the wild shoots, the Gentiles.(Rom. 11:17-24) Indeed, the Church believes that by His cross Christ, Our Peace, reconciled Jews and Gentiles, making both one in Himself(Eph. 2:14-16).[223]

Unfortunately the English translations of the New Testament often only use the generalized word "Jew" instead of the actual, specific group being referenced, i.e., the Jewish Temple Guard, the high priests,

---

223 http://www.vatican.va/archive/hist_councils/ii_vatican_council/documents/vat-ii_decl_19651028_nostra-aetate_en.html, accesses August 29, 2017.

the Pharisees, Sadducees, scribes, et al. Therefore, the unsuspecting English reader is easily misled as to the actual context and meaning being presented in the biblical passage when one reads the word "Jew." (Actually, the same is true for the word "law.")

Constantine, when he forbid the observance of Easter at Passover, at the Council of Nicaea in AD 325, declared, "It is unbecoming that on the holiest of festivals we should follow the customs of the Jews; henceforth let us have nothing in common with this odious people."[224] Sounds like something a member of the KKK or a neo-Nazi would say today. These words should never come from the mouth of a believer!

By all accounts that I have read, Constantine was not a believer. Yet, this pagan, power hungry Emperor, presided over the Council of Nicaea in AD 325. This truth should be like a bucket of cold water thrown into our faces. Sadly, in the Western world, we all "drank the cool-aid"[225] served by Constantine.

For Constantine to use the word "odious people" is referencing the Jewish population reveals a heart attitude that undoubtedly colored the decisions of this and future Church councils. To pass this off as non-sequential is to be blind to revealed truth. With the exception of only one bishop from the Eastern Church, the Council of Nicaea in AD 325 was attended by church leaders from the western portion of the Roman Empire. This created an isolated, tunnel-vision foundation for us in the Western world to build upon.

---

224 Carroll, *Constantine's Sword*, 55

225 "Drinking the Kool-Aid" is an idiom used here to refer to people that go along with an idea without questioning it.

The root of anti-Semitism can be traced all the way back to Constantine. What would have occurred if he had brought in the Jewish believers and the believers from the eastern churches to this council at Nicaea? We will never know.

Constantine sought power through control. Constantine defeated Romans Emperors Maxentius and Licinius to become sole ruler of both west and east by 324 AD.

The Council of Nicaea was held in the city of Nicaea (Turkey). Nicaea is named after "Nike, the goddess of victory."[226]

Per the Word of God, there exists a remnant today of God's chosen people. We cannot know the exact number of Israelites that are part of the remnant; only God knows who these people are. This remnant is the "true vine" we are grafted into.

> Jeremiah 50:20
> In those days and in that time, declares the LORD, iniquity shall be sought in Israel, and there shall be none, and sin in Judah, and none shall be found, for I will pardon those whom I leave as a remnant. (ESV)

Many other passages could be added, but the point is this: This "remnant" is protected by the LORD. Try as we may, they will not be deceived. History confirms that "the tradition of arguing against Jews from their own Scriptures" leads to "abysmal failure."[227]

---

226 ibid

227 Carroll, *Constantine's Sword*, 303

Genesis 9:12-13

And God said: "This is the sign of the covenant which I make between Me and you, and every living creature that is with you, for perpetual generations: I set My in the cloud, and it shall be for the sign of the covenant between Me and the earth." (NKJV)

Isaiah 54:9-10

"This is like the days of Noah to me: *as I swore that the waters of Noah should no more go over the earth, so I have sworn that I will not be angry with you, and will not rebuke you.* For the mountains may depart and the hills be removed, but my steadfast love shall not depart from you, and my covenant of peace shall not be removed," says the Lord, who has compassion on you. (ESV, italics added)

For this is like the waters of Noah to Me: Just as God promised that the flood waters of Noah's day would not cover the earth forever, so will His anger recede from Israel.

For the mountains shall depart … but My kindness shall not depart from you: Flood waters recede, and mountains do not. But even if the mountains shall depart, even if the hills be removed, the kindness of the LORD to His people will never depart. The kindness of the LORD is more certain than the mountains and the hills, and His covenant of peace is more sure.[228]

228 David Guzik, comments on Isaiah 54:9-10,

Isaiah 54:5

For your *Maker is your husband*, the LORD of hosts is his name; and *the Holy One of Israel is your Redeemer*, the God of the whole earth he is called. (ESV, italics added)

Jeremiah 35:19

Therefore this is what the LORD Almighty, the God of Israel, says: 'Jehonadab son of Rekab *will never fail to have a descendant to serve me*.'" (NIV, italics added)

As I close this chapter, the above Scriptures simply state what I have been saying with many words. First, God has a covenant with the earth and with Noah. His covenant with earth and Noah is forever. Now, this eternal covenant is used to validate, yet, another covenant noted in Isaiah 54:9-10! The Creator as the husband of Israel (Isaiah 54:5) declares that His covenant with Israel is forever (Isaiah 54:9-10).

Luke 15:1-7

Now the tax collectors and sinners were all drawing near to hear him. And the Pharisees and the scribes grumbled, saying, "This man receives sinners and eats with them." So he told them this parable: "What man of you, having a hundred sheep, if he has lost one of them, *does not leave the ninety-nine* in the open country, *and go after the one that is lost*, until he finds it? And when

---

https://www.blueletterbible.org/Comm/guzik_david/StudyGuide2017-Isa/Isa-54.cfm, accessed February 15, 2018.

> he has found it, he lays it on his shoulders, rejoicing. And when he comes home, he calls together his friends and his neighbors, saying to them, 'Rejoice with me, for I have found my sheep that was lost.' Just so, I tell you, there will be more joy in heaven over one sinner who repents than over ninety-nine righteous persons who need no repentance. (ESV, italics added)

The faithful Israelites are the "ninety-nine" (Luke 15) sheep that never left the fold! Sadly, some Western theologians have changed the Word to satisfy their own agenda.

Deception #6 - All of Israel rejected God and His Son, the Messiah

CHAPTER ELEVEN

What is Your Decision?

Many of us aren't nearly as independent-minded as we like to think. The views many of us hold are largely dictated by partisanship and ideological affiliations rather than intellectual rigor. This leads to an almost chronic unwillingness to revisit and refine long-held positions. Our thinking on matters of politics and philosophy and faith not only can become lazy; it can easily ossify. It may be worth asking yourself: in the last 15 to 20 years, on what issues of importance have you changed your mind, recalibrated your thinking, or even attempted to take a fresh look? Or has every event, serious study, a new set of facts merely confirmed what you already knew? To put it another way: do you think you're ever wrong?[229]

Here we are at the last chapter. What is Your Decision? You do have one. You can throw this book away and shout a few choice adjectives expressing your opinion of it and the author, or, you can revisit the Scriptures noted and ask the Holy Spirit, the Master Teacher (John 14:26), to speak to you about what the LORD wants you to do. The gnawing in your gut may be the probing question "Is the author right about the *End Time Deceptions*?" If so, Scripture is very clear as to your next step.

[229] Weekly magazine THE WEEK, in the section, *Viewpoint*, June 19, 2015

Jeremiah 31:19

After I strayed, I repented; after I came to understand, I beat my breast. I was ashamed and humiliated because I bore the disgrace of my youth. (NIV)

Romans 2:5

But because of your hard and impenitent heart you are storing up wrath for yourself on the day of wrath when God's righteous judgment will be revealed. (ESV)

Jeremiah 26:3

Perhaps they will listen and turn from their evil ways. Then I will change my mind about the disaster I am ready to pour out on them because of their sins. (ESV)

Revelation 2:5

Consider how far you have fallen! Repent and do the things you did at first. If you do not repent, I will come to you and remove your lampstand from its place. (NIV)

1 John 3:4

Everyone who makes a practice of sinning also practices lawlessness; sin is lawlessness.

Matthew 7:22-27

21 "Not everyone who says to me, 'Lord, Lord,' will enter the kingdom of heaven, but the one who does the will of my Father who is in heaven. 22 On that day many will say to me, 'Lord, Lord, did we not prophesy in your name, and cast out demons in your name, and do many mighty works in your name?' 23 And then will I declare to them, 'I never knew you; depart from me, you workers of lawlessness.' 24 "Everyone then who hears these words of mine and does them will be like a wise man who built his house on the rock. 25 And the rain fell, and the floods came, and the winds blew and beat on that house, but it did not fall, because it had been founded on the rock. 26 And everyone who hears these words of mine and does not do them will be like a foolish man who built his house on the sand. 27 And the rain fell, and the floods came, and the winds blew and beat against that house, and it fell, and great was the fall of it." (ESV)

As you ponder your decision, let's review the six deceptions covered in this book.

Deception #1. The Authority of the Institutional Catholic Church has usurped the authority of God. Among other things, the Institutional Church endorsed the Crusades, the Inquisition, anti-Semitism, and anti-Judaism, declaring that Christians who did not agree with their doctrine as heretics, declaring that "that outside of her [the Church institution] there is neither salvation nor the remission of sin",[230] and the embracing of the title *Vicar of Christ* by the Pope, et al. These actions collectively, in effect, make the Church's authority above the Bible.

Deception #2 - The Sabbath - The Word of God teaches us to observe the seventh day. The Sabbath has been replaced with Sunday, a pagan day of worship of the Sun god. This is direct disobedience of the fourth of the Ten Commandments.

Deception #3 - Arrangement of the Bible changed - The order of the Bible was changed to meet man's desire over the historically accepted order for God's Word. Even the Messiah endorsed the historic, Hebrew arrangement of the Bible.

Deception #4 – The arrogance of thinking that, "My hands are clean as I stand before the LORD and that I am okay with status quo." Those under this deception are found in the words of Isaiah 29:13, "The Lord says: 'These people come near to me with their mouth and honor me with their lips, but their hearts are far from me. Their worship of me is based on merely human rules they have been taught.'" (NIV) Jesus spoke these words from Isaiah in Mark chapter seven when He charged the religious leaders with observing the traditions made by men. Jesus called these people "hypocrites" (Mark 7:6). The heart of a hypocrite is a person who wears the mask and acts as if he or she is a follower of God and His Word. These individuals are very quick to judge others, all the while never looking at their own self-centered lives (Matthew 7:3-5). Hypocrisy is a choice one makes. In Mark 7:8, Jesus says that you have "let go of the commands of God

230 Carroll, *Constantine's Sword*, 315

and are holding on to the traditions of men" and in verse 13, "you nullify the word of God by your traditions" (NIV). When a person nullifies the Word found in the whole Bible, he or she basically declares that these Words of God are no longer relevant today. Since the Word became flesh (John 1:14), to reject the Bible is in fact a rejection of the Messiah (Jesus).

Deception #5 - Adopting an historical anti-Semitic, anti-Judaist attitude. Part of this deception is the fact that the primary reason Jewish people today do not even discuss the possibility that Jesus is the Messiah is due, in part, to our own anti-Semitic attitude towards them. In short, it is our arrogance. Yes, we may have inherited this historically negative attitude towards the Jews and/or Israel, but to not repent of this racial attitude is sin.

Deception #6 - All of Israel rejected God and His Son, the Messiah. This, of course would not be so widely believed without Deception #5. A major course correction was made when Pope Paul VI declared within the *Nostra Aetate* that the eternal covenant between God and the People of Israel has not been broken. Hopefully, we Gentiles Christians can make a similar course correction.

As I leave you to ponder this matter with your heavenly Father, may the following Scriptures be useful to you.

Isaiah 54:5

For thy Maker is thine husband; the LORD of hosts is his name; and thy Redeemer the Holy One of Israel; The God of the whole earth shall he be called. (KJV)

Isaiah 41:14

Fear not, you worm Jacob, you men of Israel! I am the one who helps you, declares the LORD; your Redeemer is the Holy One of Israel.

Isaiah 43:1-11

1 But now thus says the LORD, he who created you, O Jacob, he who formed you, O Israel: "Fear not, for I have redeemed you; I have called you by name, you are mine. 2 When you pass through the waters, I will be with you; and through the rivers, they shall not overwhelm you; when you walk through fire you shall not be burned, and the flame shall not consume you. 3 For I am the LORD your God, the Holy One of Israel, your Savior. I give Egypt as your ransom, Cush and Seba in exchange for you. 4 Because you are precious in my eyes, and honored, and I love you, I give men in return for you, peoples in exchange for your life. 5 Fear not, for I am with you; I will bring your offspring from the east, and from the west I will gather you. 6 I will say to the north, Give up, and to the south, Do not withhold; bring my sons from afar and my daughters from the end of the earth, 7 everyone who is called by my name, whom I created for my glory, whom I formed and made." 8 Bring out the people who are blind, yet have eyes, who are deaf, yet have ears! 9 All the nations gather together, and the peoples assemble. Who among them can declare this, and show us the former things? Let them bring their witnesses

to prove them right, and let them hear and say, It is true. 10 "You are my witnesses," declares the LORD, "and my servant whom I have chosen, that you may know and believe me and understand that I am he. Before me no god was formed, nor shall there be any after me. 11 I, I am the LORD, and besides me there is no savior. (ESV)

2 Timothy 3:16

All Scripture (all of the *Tanakh*) is breathed out by God and profitable for teaching, for reproof, for correction, and for training in righteousness (ESV, italics added).

1 John 3:6

No one who abides in him keeps on sinning; no one who keeps on sinning has either seen him or known him. (ESV)

1 John 2:3

And by this we know that we have come to know him, *if we keep his commandments*. (ESV, italics added)

Dear friend, do not let yourself slip into eternity *hoping* that you obeyed God's Word found in the Bible. There is no gray area. You either are walking in obedience or you are walking in sin. Jesus said in 1 Peter 1:16, "Be holy, because I am holy." This is NOT some intellectual or philosophical holiness. This is NOT about having the right doctrine.

This is about obedience. This is the day to make things right between you and your Creator. He has sent His Son as your Savior. His Spirit is waiting to give you strength and understanding. Lay aside Western-Greek based thinking and take up a mindset that is aligned with the Bible; the mindset of Christ.

Why is this important? (1) Your own personal eternal security and (2) John 4:35, "Do you not say, 'There are yet four months, then comes the harvest'? Look, I tell you, lift up your eyes, and see that the fields are white for harvest" (ESV).

> I am grateful for Dr. Reilly's extensive research and dedication to uncovering God's truths which have been distorted by the schemes of Satan in ways in which most of us, especially in the Western church, have been completely unaware.
>
> Considering the dualism of Greek thought compared to the non-dualism of Hebrew thought, I realize that being a Christian is not defined by what you believe, but by who you are: truly a new creation in Christ. This gives II Corinthians 5:17 even greater clarity to me.
>
> After being made aware of deceptions currently in place, the question becomes: How will this knowledge affect our lives?
>
> **Cynthia Hobbs Baker**

APPENDIX A

A Biblical Worldview

A biblical worldview is a comprehensive conception of the world from a standpoint based upon the whole Bible; not only the Old or New Testaments.

Your worldview is an amalgamation of one's secular and biblical beliefs melded together into a single view of the world.

Our worldview is our reality (whether it is based upon truth or lies). Therefore, our worldview is the foundation upon which all else in life is built.

A flaw in one's biblical worldview has eternal consequences.

In the Bible, we read passages like the one in Matthew 5:27, "*You have heard that it was said,*"'"(NIV, italics added). Of course, this statement, "*You have heard that it was said*" is referring to what the hearers had heard over the years; the teachings of the *Tanakh.*[231]

When we hear a teaching in a local church, at times, the statement made or the worldview, perhaps unconsciously, expressed by

231 The *Tanakh* is the Hebrew Bible (what is also called *The Old Testament*).

the speaker may not be fully or clearly supported by either the Old or New Testaments. How often do you follow-up study of the sermon to validate that what was taught is actually what the Bible says? If the hearer is only passively listening, he or she may not notice anything wrong in the message. Nonetheless, the hearer has been shaped by the sermon's message. When this occurs, the hearer is ripe for deception.

Apathy is the doorway through which deception freely enters.

At times, the forces that shape the opinions presented from our pulpits are the views and values of our Western culture, which, at times, have a regional and/or denominational emphasis. Being in line with the denomination's views does not mean or imply that the message is completely biblical.

Biblical truth transcends all cultures over the span of time.

Yes, we are all affected by the opinions expressed by leadership in our local churches. Also, many of us have an inherited worldview. For example, some have a worldview passed down from parents or the community in which you grew up. The point is that everyone has a worldview, even though you may never think about it using this terminology. If you were asked to verbalize your world view, like most people, you may have difficulty expressing it in a concise way. Still, you have a worldview! The challenge to us is to make sure that we have a biblical worldview.

Why the focus on our worldviews, when the topic of this book is about *End Time Deception*? My concern is with the unspoken values and beliefs that govern our lives that are buried in our worldviews. For example, in over 90% of the local churches in which I have ministered, which crosses many denomination, there are several understood attitudes, values or opinions held by the congregation that do not 100% align with the teachings of the Bible. Since these non-biblical attitudes are byproducts of one's worldview, they lack objectivity in self-evaluation. Of course, true self objectivity is found in allowing the LORD to freely search one's heart. It is found when we compare our life-style against the Bible.

> Psalm 139:23-24
> Search me, O God, and know my heart! Try me and know my thoughts [my cares]! And see if there be any grievous way in me, and lead me in the way everlasting (in the ancient way)! (ESV)

Allow me to further explain the point being made by asking a few questions:

(1) Is your local church's congregation comprised of mostly Caucasians from Western European countries?
(2) What percentage of the congregation is of a different ethnic orientation?

(3) If you are part of a mostly Caucasian congregation, would individuals from African, Latin, or Asian descent be fully embraced and welcomed to join your church?

(4) What if your local church is mostly African-American or Asian? How many Caucasians are in your church's community?

(5) Now, the real question is what part of your worldview has allowed for this "judgement of other ethnics groups" to exist when it is clearly against the teaching of the Bible?

1 John 2:9
Whoever says, "I am in the light," while hating a brother or sister, is still in the darkness. (NRSV)

Yes, I understand that you are not prejudice against other ethnic groups. I know that you would surely welcome other ethnic groups into your church. Look, we are as separated theologically as we are separated racially. Yet, there is only one Bible that contains one truth.

The fact of the matter is that your current opinion of other ethnic groups, or the Old Testament, or Israel (the descendants of Abraham, Isaac, and Jacob), or the institution we call "the Church," or "salvation," and what it means to "obey God's Word" are all influenced more by your worldview than from rigorous study of the Bible!

Your initial response may be, "So what? I know that Christ is my Savior and that when I die I am going to heaven." My response is this, "What if you are wrong? Where is the proof for what you claim?"

These seemingly trivial matters are major matters according to the Bible. Yes, your Christian community may agree with you and even support your views, but if your views are not 100% aligned with God's Word, then you are living a lie.

Think about this most serious situation for one moment. Why? Because you will not fully know where you stand, eternally speaking, until after you have breathed your last breath! Your physical body is dead and your soul and spirit step into eternity. What does the Bible say about what takes place after death? Oh yes, "And just as it is appointed for man to die once, and after that comes judgment" (ESV, Hebrews 9:27).

Again I ask, "What if you are wrong?"

Do you not think for one minute that you have been deceived on some eternal theological point? Do you really believe that your worldview is 100% based upon the Word of God?

The fact of the matter is that there are no groups in eternity called Methodists, or Baptists, or Pentecostals.

Since "judgement" is included in one of the elementary teachings of the Christian faith (Hebrews 6:1-2) we should not treat this matter too casually.

The work of the "false Prophets" mentioned in Matthew 7:15 are very good at their job. What is their job? Deceiving believers like you and me! The text in Matthew could not give us a clearer warning.

> Matthew 7:13, 14, 21
>
> "Enter by the narrow gate. For the gate is wide and the way is easy that leads to destruction, and those who enter by it are many. For the gate is narrow and the way is hard that leads to life, and those who find it are few…Not everyone who says to me, 'Lord, Lord,' will enter the kingdom of heaven, but the one who does the will of my Father who is in heaven" (ESV).

These individuals are calling Christ, "Lord, Lord." Although they are addressing Him as the divine Lord, and although these individuals may have done many things in Jesus' name, they utterly failed the critical test: *They did not do the will of the Father.*

If your worldview is flawed, spiritually speaking, and you have not diligently searched the Word of God through the power of the Holy Spirit in order to modify incorrect thinking and behavior, then you are playing Russian roulette with your eternal life.

APPENDIX B

What the Church Should Look Like

1. Baptized with the Holy Spirit
2. They devoted themselves to the apostles' teaching
3. They were devoted to fellowship
4. They were devoted to the breaking of bread and the prayers
5. They were devoted to praying
6. Many wonders and signs were being done
7. All who believed were together and had all things in common
8. They met day by day, attending the temple together and breaking bread in their homes
9. They received their food with glad and generous hearts
10. They were praising God
11. The Lord added to their number day by day those who were being saved
12. They were of one heart and soul
13. No one said that any of the things that belonged to him was his own, but they had everything in common
14. Great grace was upon them all
15. There was not a needy person among them
16. The proceeds of what was sold was distributed to each as any had need
17. None of the non-believers dared join them

18. The non-believers held the believers in high esteem
19. The sick were all healed
20. Those afflicted with unclean spirits, and they were all healed

APPENDIX C

Further Discussion on the Authority of the Institutional Church

Early in my marriage I recall once when Jean and I decided to leave the church in which we had attended for a few years. Within a few days of our leaving, we received more than one phone call from friends at that church. Their message was simple: by leaving that particular local church we had "lost our salvation."

Questions:

- I have wondered what would have happened if this particular church had had the same power and authority of the Church in the thirteenth century. Would Jean and I have been burned at the stake?
- Have we lost our intimacy and the personal relationship with the Father, Son and Holy Spirit?
- Has our intimacy and the personal relationship with the Father, Son and Holy Spirit been replaced, or at least watered down, by a relationship with an organization that we call Church?

- Have we bound the Holy Spirit with the traditions of the Church we attend? Let your service run over the allotted time and see what happens. Or, more to the point, move one of the sacred articles from the sanctuary and wait for the fireworks.
- Is the Holy Spirit truly free to move in our midst?

Allow me to touch on finances. When it comes to finding out what the Bible says about any topic, it is best to go to the actual Bible first and last, instead of asking people for their opinions!

Today, what saddens me most is that we build great monuments to the LORD made of wood, stone and other perishables. We call these monuments Churches. We usually add personal affection when we call it, "My Church." We should be investing into the lives of our brothers and sisters, and in reaching the Lost!

The thing of it is, when we "invest" in a building, by default, we then have a vested interest in the building. If we invest a lot into the building, over time, we have a sense of ownership. It becomes more and more "my church." All the while, our "good works" are taking us further and further from the LORD and His Word.

> Acts 11:27-29
>
> At that time prophets came down from Jerusalem to Antioch. One of them named Agabus stood up and predicted by the Spirit that there would be a severe famine over all the world; and this took place during the reign of Claudius. The disciples

determined that according to their ability, each would send relief to the believers living in Judea (NRSV).

There was a need, so they simply met the need.

Malachi 3:10

Bring the full tithe into the storehouse, so that there may be food in my house, and thus put me to the test, says the Lord of hosts; see if I will not open the windows of heaven for you and pour down for you an overflowing blessing. (NRSV)

Acts 4:34-35

There was not a needy person among them, for as many as owned lands or houses sold them and brought the proceeds of what was sold. They laid it at the apostles' feet, and it was distributed to each as any had need. (NRSV)

The "storehouse" was a public storehouse (Nehemiah 13: 10-13) that was akin to what we see in Acts 4, and that the Apostles saw that there was not any needy person among them.

During the time of the Temple, the purpose of financial donations was twofold: (1) To take care of the Levites who cared for the Temple and (2) for the poor.

Usually, people do not give what they should because they do not trust God. They, like Cain, give "some." This is revealed in the age old question: "Do I tithe on the gross or the net on my paycheck?" Does this have to be asked?

Remember: Our Protestant churches are really modeled after the Catholic Church.

> Matthew 7:21
> "Not everyone who says to me, 'Lord, Lord,' will enter the kingdom of heaven, but the one who does the will of my Father who is in heaven." (ESV)

The influence of false prophets is very real. Be careful. I am speaking about one's eternal security! It makes no difference what you believe! If it is not the will of the Father, which is found ONLY in the Bible, then you may hear Jesus say, "…'I never knew you; depart from me, you workers of lawlessness.'"[232]

> James 4:4-5
> Adulterers! Do you not know that friendship with the world is enmity with God? Therefore whoever wishes to be a friend of the world becomes an enemy of God. Or do you suppose that it is for nothing that the scripture says, "God yearns jealously for the spirit that he has made to dwell in us"? (NRSV)

Hebraically, an "adulterous people" includes those who worship or place greater dedication to anything or person other than the one true

232 Matthew 7:23, ESV

God. When one's affection is overly tied to the local church, rather than to God and His Word, then this opens the door for the "Christian" to operate to a greater degree in one's emotions rather than in the spirit.

APPENDIX D

Zacchaeus – The Rest of the Story

At times we lack understanding of *Torah* which may open the door for incorrect interpretation of another later text. Let's look at Luke 19 and the story about Zacchaeus. Zacchaeus' Hebrew name is *Zakkai*, which means innocent.

> Luke 19:5-10
>
> And when Jesus came to the place, he looked up and said to him, "Zacchaeus, hurry and come down, for I must stay at your house today." So he hurried and came down and received him joyfully. And when they saw it, they all grumbled, "He has gone in to be the guest of a man who is a sinner." And Zacchaeus stood and said to the Lord, "Behold, Lord, the half of my goods I give to the poor. And if I have defrauded anyone of anything, I restore it fourfold." And Jesus said to him, "Today salvation has come to this house, since he also is a son of Abraham. For the Son of Man came to seek and to save the lost." (ESV)

Zacchaeus stood and said to the Lord, "Look, Lord, I give half of my goods to the poor; and if I have taken anything from anyone by false accusation, I restore fourfold." (Luke 19:8)

Torah required the amount taken, plus a 20 percent penalty in cases where the person confessed in taking money (Leviticus 6:1-5; Numbers 5:5-7).

When the thief was caught and did not show remorse, the penalty was double (Exodus 22:3).

A thief stealing what is essential and did not show pity was required to pay back fourfold (Exodus 22:1; 2 Samuel 12:6).

Zacchaeus imposed upon himself the greater penalty. His willingness to obey *Torah* led the Messiah to state that Zacchaeus was now restored in verse 9.

Zacchaeus' action was his repentance! Repentance without action is not biblical repentance.

In this story about Zacchaeus we have restoration of an Israeli by obedience to *Torah*; not via a "profession of faith" but repentance for disobeying *Torah*. Zacchaeus is covered by the top line of the Abrahamic Covenant!

And Jesus said to him, "Today salvation has come to this house, because he also is a son of Abraham; for the Son of Man has come to seek and to save that which was lost." (Luke 19:9-10)

Zacchaeus was restored to God through repentance. As the Messiah (Jesus) said to him, "Today salvation has come to this house…" Not tomorrow. Not after the resurrection. "Today", at that very moment, "salvation" came in Zacchaeus' home. How does this story align with what you have been taught about salvation in the New Testament?

> Ezekiel 34:15-16
>
> I myself will be the shepherd of my sheep, and I myself will make them lie down, declares the Lord GOD. I will seek the lost, and I will bring back the strayed, and I will bind up the injured, and I will strengthen the weak, and the fat and the strong I will destroy. I will feed them in justice. (ESV)

Who is speaking in Ezekiel 34:16? , it is God (YHWH) who seeks out the Lost Sheep of the top line of the Abrahamic Covenant.

APPENDIX E

Followers of the Way

When were the followers of the Messiah first called Christians? "…And in Antioch the disciples were first called Christians." Before this event, they were called the "followers of the Way" (Acts 22:4). Later, in the city of Antioch the name was changed.

It seems that it was the non-believing community that called the people of the Way, Christians. By doing this, calling them "Christians," revealed that *the community saw that these people were living and doing what the Messiah did.*

The people in Antioch noticed that the people of the Way obeyed the teachings of the *Tanakh* (the Jewish Bible as the New Testament did not exist) and the Messiah as if it was their vocation to do so. Today we call a person who works with electricity an electrician in that it designates the person's trade or vocation. In similar manner these first followers of the Messiah did so as it was their vocation.

I really doubt that the American, non-church-attending community would refer to us active churchgoers as people that follow the teachings of the Bible and the Messiah as our vocation. Why is that?

Have you ever asked someone if they were a Christian? Did he or she respond by saying something about their relationship to a local church or denominational affiliation? That's like saying I am a surfer because I have an article of clothing with O'Neill embossed on it. I have a granddaughter who is a surfer. What is important to my granddaughter is getting into the water with her board and catching the right wave; actually surfing. The fact of it is: to be a Christian you need to walk with God. This is done by obeying the imperatives in the Bible; not only a few commands that agree with your personal doctrine or theology. You have to actually walk as Jesus walked!

Being called a Christian associates you with the Messiah. Over the last two millennia, the name "Christian" has all but lost any real meaning. Sadly, I personally have zero confidence in anyone that identifies themselves as being a Christian when we first meet. Why? It does not tell me anything about the person! It does not tell me the person's relationship with God the Father, His Son, the Holy Spirit, or the Bible. The true Christians I know live life in such a way that their life shows others that they follow the Messiah, His Father, are filled with the Holy Spirit, and have lifestyle knowledge of the Bible.

> Hebrews 5:1
> "For though by this time you ought to be teachers, you need someone to teach you again the basic principles of the oracles of God. You need milk, not solid food" (ESV).

The teaching of the material in this book is not milk but meat. This is a teaching that has the potential of turning your theological world on its head. It does not matter how long you have attended your church. Longevity in church attendance is not a litmus test for one's relationship with the Father, Son and Holy Spirit. Just last year my wife shared Christ with a lady that had been a member of a Protestant church for over sixty years. Yet, she did not know that she needed a relationship with Christ for salvation. She assumed church membership was all that was needed.

> Matthew 7:21-24
> "Not everyone who *says to me, 'Lord, Lord,'* will enter the kingdom of heaven, but the one who does the *will of my Father* who is in heaven. On that day many will say to me, 'Lord, Lord, did we not prophesy in your name, and cast out demons in your name, and *do many mighty works in your name*?' And then will I declare to them, '*I never knew you; depart from me, you workers of lawlessness.*' "Everyone then who *hears these words* of mine and *does them* will be like a wise man who built his house on the rock. (ESV, italics added)

This may seem like I am repeating myself - I am because this is so critical. The words, "*Lord, Lord*" are words that many Christians may actually say in reference to Christ, yet words alone, or even church membership, are not enough to secure one's eternal salvation from the penalty of sin.[233] If *saying a few words* was all that was required, *then* the Lord would **not** have added the condition about *doing the Father's will.* If salvation was only about saying things, then God could have summed

233 Granted, in a deathbed confession, words are all the dying person has to offer. I assume that readers are not in such a dire situation.

this up in a few paragraphs on a postcard, instead of giving us the entire Bible. I'm not being facetious.

How do you objectively quantify that you are a true follower of the LORD God?

When I put salt and pepper on my food I do not use empty salt and pepper shakers. Matthew 5: 13-14 tells us that we are the salt and the lights so that people may see "our good deeds"; see us living out the words of the Bible.

If those who proclaim, and really meant, that the Father was the absolute authority in their lives by declaring *Lord, Lord*, they would have done the "*will of my Father*." The will of the Father is not synonymous with doing the will of your pastor or following the traditions of your local church. (This statement is fundamental to our understanding of *End Time Deception*.)

It does not matter what a person has said or done in God's name, or Jesus' name, or even in the name of the Holy Spirit, or the church's name, if it was not birthed from a heart that is fully surrendered to the Father and the Son as the absolute owner of the person's life.

Scripture teaches that we should be honest with our words. Matthew 5:37, "Let what you say be simply 'Yes' or 'No'; anything more than this comes from evil" (ESV). Some pastors and missionaries I have known over the years that "agreed" (said "Yes") in their respective denominational statements (in order to not lose their ordination with the denomination), yet told me privately that they did not agree with the documents they signed. Often, our concern for man's approval is done at the risk of disobeying God's Word.

We are all too familiar with "Christianity as a religion" which is often centered on the activities of a local church. As we have seen, this was, in part, the effect of the *End Time Deception.*

Religion is "the belief in and worship of a superhuman controlling power, especially a personal God or gods."[234] Using this definition, Christianity can be classified as a religion. Yet, in a biblical sense, Christianity is not a religion because it is based upon a relationship between people and God the Father, His Son, the Holy Spirit, and the Bible.

What Matthew (7:21-24, quoted earlier) addresses is the reality that God alone is the One that gives us, His followers, our daily marching orders (which is His will for our lives).

God has no partners! If He did, then He would not ask us to call Him Lord![235] The individuals that *only serve God with their words and/or their religious activities* at "their church" may hear Jesus say, "*I never knew you; depart from me, you workers of lawlessness"* (Matthew 7:23, ESV).

"Lawlessness" has two faces. On one hand it is the open disregard for God's written Word. On the other, it places the person's will where we should find God's will.

---

234 https://en.oxforddictionaries.com/definition/religion, accessed October 11, 2017.

235 See Romans 8:15, 10:9. God is our Father and Jesus is our friend. This does not devalue the biblical fact that He is LORD.

We have to both hear the Word *and* do the Word (His will). If not, we are guilty of being lawless in the eyes of God.

> I finished reading your newest book, *End Time Deception is Here.* I am still trying to digest all the tremendous research and scholarly application. It is well done to say the least. It certainly has opened my eyes to the deceptions that have plagued the church for centuries and explains the current state of the church.
>
> Pastor Don Milner
> Radiant Life Church

APPENDIX F

Perilous Times[236]

2 Timothy 3:1

"But know this, that in the *last days* perilous times will come." (NKJV, italics added)

2 Timothy 3:1

"Moreover, understand this: in the *acharit-hayamim*[237] will come *trying times*." (CJB, italics added)

Trivia: *Acharit HaYamim* (bə·'a·ḥă·rîṯ hay·yā·mîm) basically means, the "end of days." As we will see on the following pages, another Jewish term, *olam hazeh* (oh-lahm haz-ZEH), refers to "the present age."

If we view the Bible only through a Western-Greek cultural lens, we may miss the deeper meaning of the text at hand. Concerning the above passage in Second Timothy, there is some debate about the actual time period covered in the statement found in Second Timothy 3:1: "in the last days" (*acharit-hayamim*). In the context of Paul's letter,

---

236 Drawn from my book, *The Master's Model*, (Columbia: Create Space Publishing, 2016), 31-42.

237 *Acharit HaYamim* is a Hebrew term used in Jewish eschatology and means "end of days" or "the last days" (eschatology deals with the final events in the history of the world or of humankind).

the "last days" refers to the period of the Great Tribulation just before Yeshua (Jesus) returns to establish His Kingdom. These "last days" are not a single moment in time; they will span a period of years. The "last days" will be preceded by a buildup that will reach its fullest height during the end of this time of tribulation.

Many, including myself, acknowledge that we are "in the last days" and that is why I am passionate about awakening the sleeping giant; church-goers who live their lives in such a way that following Christ is more a philosophical concept or religious obligation than a living reality.

Many church-goers have created a pseudo-Christianity that is a shadow of the life of the believers spoken about in the Bible. For them, following Christ is summed up by attending the activities at a local church that they enjoy. To varying degrees, doing so is but one of the many mundane obligations on their weekly to-do lists. For these individuals, the concept of Matthew 16:24 is just more words found in the Bible.

> Matthew 16:24
> "Then said Jesus unto his disciples, If any man [or woman] will come after me, let him deny himself, and take up his cross, and follow me." (KJV)

Where are you in regard to Matthew 16:24?

> Matthew 24:3
>
> "When he was sitting on the Mount of Olives, the talmidim came to him privately. 'Tell us,' they said, 'when will these things happen? And what will be the sign that you are coming, and that the 'olam hazeh is ending?'" (CJB)

> Matthew 24:3
>
> "And as he sat upon the mount of Olives, the disciples came unto him privately, saying, Tell us, when shall these things be? and what shall be the sign of thy coming, and of the end of the world?" (KJV)

The wording in the *Complete Jewish Bible* differs from the *King James Version* only with the usage of the original language expressions "*talmidim*" and "*olam hazeh.*" As previously stated, the *talmidim* is the Hebrew word for Jesus' disciples. The expression *olam hazeh* (oh-lahm haz-ZEH) refers to the present age.

The present age is the time between the fall of Adam and the return of the Messiah. The return of the Messiah may not be the same event when the Groom (Jesus) comes for His Bride (the Church), which may occur as much as seven years before the return of the

Messiah. "According to the Sages[238] the *Olam Hazzh* will endure for 6,000 years."[239] Therefore, the present age is rapidly coming to an end.

> 2 Timothy 3:1-9
>
> "But know this, that *in the last days perilous times will come*: For men will be lovers of themselves, lovers of money, boasters, proud, blasphemers, disobedient to parents, unthankful, unholy, unloving, unforgiving, slanderers, without self-control, brutal, despisers of good, traitors, headstrong, haughty, lovers of pleasure rather than lovers of God, *having a form of godliness but denying its power*. And from such people turn away! For of this sort are those who creep into households and make captives of gullible women loaded down with sins, led away by various lusts, always learning and never able to come to the knowledge of the truth. Now as Jannes and Jambres[240] resisted Moses, so do these also resist the truth: men of corrupt minds, disapproved concerning the faith; but they will progress no further, for their folly will be manifest to all, as theirs also was." (NKJV, italics added)

---

238 In the days of Jeremiah and Ezekiel (Jeremiah 18:18; Ezekiel 7:26) three distinct classes of teachers were recognized by the people: prophets, priests, and wise men or sages.

239 Hebrew for Christians, accessed December 11, 2015, http://www.hebrew4christians.com/Glossary O.

240 Jewish tradition says that Jannes and Jambres were the two chief magicians who resisted Moses and Aaron (Exodus 7:10-12; 22; 8:7, 19) and that they left Egypt with the Israelites. In like manner, there will be those who resist godly leaders today.

The question presented by the disciples to Jesus (in Matthew 24:3) may seem to be twofold, yet it is one single question: "What shall be the sign of thy coming [Christ's return as the Groom coming for His Bride], and of the end of the world (*olam hazeh*) as we know it?

> 2 Timothy 3:1
>
> "But know this, that *in the last days perilous times will come*:" (NKJV, italics added)

The "perilous times" mentioned by the Paul is stated as a fact. In other words, like it or not, perilous times are going to be our reality; this truth is not an option.

In traditional Jewish eschatology, human history is usually divided into three distinct epochs[241] of 2,000 years. Generally, these three epochs are known in Judism as "*tohu*, [242] *Torah*, [243] and *yemot ha-mashiah*."[244] The three epochs are (1) "chaos/disorder", followed by (2) "the period of the *Torah*," and finally the (3) "days of the Messiah." [245]

The Herodian Temple was officially destroyed in AD 70. However, the God-given authority and role of the physical temple in

---

241 *Epoch* is a period of time that is very important in history (Merriam-Webster).

242 *Tohu* means chaos or disorder. The Hebrew word *tohu* also means "without form" as in Genesis 1:2, "the earth was without form."

243 The epoch of *Torah* refers to the period of time when Israel started to live according to the teachings and instructions received from God.

244 *Yemot* means days. *Ha-mashiah* means the Messiah. *Yemot ha-mashiah* means the days of the Messiah.

245 Shubert Spero, *Holocaust and Return to Zion: A Study in Jewish Philosophy of History* (Hoboken: KTAV Publishing House, Inc., 2000), 105.

Jerusalem, the Cohanim,[246] the Levites, and animal sacrifices would come to an end with the destruction of the Temple in Jerusalem. A new epoch most likely began when Christ said "it is finished" (John 19:30). However, the covenant God made with Abraham and the descendants of Aaron was an everlasting covenant (Genesis 12:1-3; Exodus 19:5–6; Numbers 25:13; Isaiah 60:1–3). Yes, this covenant had conditions, as does the covenant God makes with the non-Israeli nations. The everlasting covenant God made with Abraham and the descendants of Aaron is a theological mystery. Apparently, it is not for you and me to fully understand God's relationship with historical Israel. Speculate as we may, the truth is this: God honors His everlasting covenants. Based on 1 Kings 19:18[247] and Romans 11:3-5,[248] it is God alone that has preserved a people that will worship Him.[249]

Before the first temple was built by Solomon, worship took place in the tabernacle (a tent), which is called "the temple of the Lord" (1 Samuel

---

246 "Jewish tradition, based on the *Torah*, is that all Cohanim are direct descendants of Aaron, the brother of Moses. The Cohen line is patrilineal -- passed from father to son without interruption for 3,300 years, or more than 100 generations." (Source: Aish.com, accessed October 18, 2016, http://www.aish.com/ci/sam/48936742.html.

In Judaism, the Cohanim are those who qualify to serve as High Priest. During the time of Christ, this practiced was replaced with a corrupt system that was heavily influenced by the Roman government and powerful Jewish leaders.

247 1 Kings 19:18 (NIV), "Yet I reserve seven thousand in Israel--all whose knees have not bowed down to Baal and whose mouths have not kissed him."

248 Romans 11:3-5 (NIV), 3 "Lord, they have killed your prophets and torn down your altars; I am the only one left, and they are trying to kill me"? 4 And what was God's answer to him? "I have reserved for myself seven thousand who have not bowed the knee to Baal."5 So too, at the present time there is a remnant chosen by God.

249 For example, in Jeremiah 25:19, God makes an eternal promise to "Jonadab son of Recab". The promise God made to his family was this: Your family "will never fail to have a man to serve" Him. Therefore, even today there are descendants of Jonadab that serve God.

1:9). The temple erected by Solomon was damaged in war during the course of its history. It was finally destroyed by Nebuchadnezzar (2 Kings 24:13; 2 Chronicles 36:7). After the return from captivity, Israel, under Zerubbabel and the high priest Jeshua, construction began to rebuild the temple. The temple was completed under the prophets Haggai and Zechariah (Ezra 5: 6-17; 6:1-15). It was ready for consecration in the spring of 516 BC, twenty years after the return from captivity. The temple erected by the exiles on their return from Babylon had stood for about five hundred years, when Herod the Great became king of Judea. The temple had suffered considerably from natural decay and from numerous wars. Herod, desiring to gain the favor of the Jewish people, proposed to rebuild it. Reconstruction began in 18 BC and was completed in AD 65.

The first epoch is referred to as *tohu.* It is also called the epoch of chaos or disorder. This first epoch occurred from the time of "the fall of Adam until the call of Abraham." [250]

The epoch of *Torah* occurred from "Abraham until the time of the destruction of the Second Temple." [251]

The final epoch is called the *Days of the Messiah* and refers to the time "when the Messiah could appear." At the end of the final epoch, Christ will set up His Kingdom in Zion.[252]

---

250 Hebrew for Christians, accessed December 11, 2015, http://www.hebrew4christians.com/Articles/Perilous_ Times/ perilous_times.html.

251 Ibid.

252 Ibid.

> Abraham marked the transition from the period of Tohu to the period of Torah, or Tikun (since the rectification of reality can occur only through the Torah). Although the Torah was not actually given until 448 years after this, the sages state that the forefathers (under Godly leadership) kept the entire Torah before it was given, and the creation of the Jewish people that began with Abraham was the preparation for the giving of the Torah in written form. Thus, the period of Torah can justifiably be considered to have begun with Abraham.[253]

Trivia: Many scholars and historians date Jesus' crucifixion to either Friday April 7, AD 30 or Friday, April 3, AD 33. Matthew, Mark, and Luke each record that Jesus died about "the ninth hour"[254] (Matthew 27:45-50, Mark 15:34-37, Luke 23:44-46). Therefore, if we conclude that the end of the second epoch (the period of *Torah*) ended with Jesus saying "…*It is finished*," and he bowed his head and gave up his spirit" in John 19:30 (ESV, italics added), then, if one of these dates in April marks the end of the second 2,000 year epoch (the period of the *Torah*), and not to the actual date the Herodian temple was destroyed (AD 70), then this third and last 2,000 year epoch (days of the Messiah) will end in the year of 2030 or 2033 (14-17 years from today in 2016).[255]

---

253 Chabad.org, accessed December 14, 2015,.http://www.chabad.org/kabbalah/article_cdo/aid/ 583722/jewish/Sparks-in-Sodom-Part-1.htm.

254 The ninth hour is 3:00 pm. Keep in mind that the Sabbath begins at sundown on Friday (between 3:00 and 6:00 pm).

255 The Jewish New Year 5777 (*Rosh Hashana*) started at sunset on Monday, October 3, 2016, Jerusalem time. According to tradition, God created Adam and Eve on October 7, 3761 BC (3761 + 2016=5777). Try as we may, we will never calculate the day the Messiah will return. Therefore, the Epoch of the Messiah may occur in our lifetime or it may not occur for another couple of hundred years.

Israel became a nation once again in 1948 after being dispersed around the world for almost 2,000 years.[256]

> According to many of the sages, the time immediately preceding the appearance (return) of the Messiah (the end of the last 2,000 [year] epoch) will be a time of testing in which the world will undergo various forms of tribulation - the "birth pangs of the Messiah." Some say the birth pangs are to last for 70 years, with the last 7 years being the most intense period of tribulation. This is called the "Time of Jacob's Trouble" (Jeremiah 30:7). The climax of the Great Tribulation is called the great "Day of the LORD" which represents God's wrath poured out upon a rebellious world system. On this day, the LORD will shake the entire earth (Isaiah 2:19) and worldwide calamities will occur. "For the great day of their wrath has come, and who can stand?" (Revelation 6:17). The prophet Malachi likewise says: "'Surely the day is coming; it will burn like a furnace. All the arrogant and every evildoer will be stubble, and that day that is coming will set them on fire,' says the LORD Almighty. 'Not a root or a branch will be left to them'" (Malachi 4:1). Only after the nations of the world have been judged will the Messianic kingdom be established upon the earth.[257]

Make no mistake, we, especially in the Western World, are living in a self-absorbed, self-created pseudo-Christian world.

---

256 Israel became a nation at midnight May 14th, 1948. Israel becoming a nation fulfilled such prophecies as Ezekiel 36 and 37 and signaled the soon end of the age (of the Messiah). During the Six Day War, June 5-10, 1967, the temple mount was captured along with east Jerusalem by Israel.

257 Hebrew for Christians, accessed December 11, 2015, http://www.hebrew4christians.com/Articles/Perilous_ Times/ perilous_times.html.

In Second Timothy 3:2-5, Paul provides a list of characteristics that will reflect the hearts of people during this final period of human history (the last 70 years of this epoch). "People will be lovers of self, lovers of money, proud, arrogant, abusive, disobedient to their parents, ungrateful, unholy, heartless, unappeasable, slanderous, without self-control, brutal, not loving good, treacherous, reckless, swollen with conceit, lovers of pleasure rather than lovers of God, having the appearance of godliness, but denying its power." Instead of loving God, we are "lovers of [ourselves]," "lovers of money," "lovers of pleasure more than lovers of God," and "not lovers of good." Godless self-centeredness has become the norm in our society and in many of our local churches.

Depending on the degree of deception one has been exposed to, these perilous times are taking a powerful toll on us (who have been called to "go and make disciples"). An active church-goer may say, "My church has not been affected. I have not been deceived! I do not know what you are talking about?" My reply, "When was the last time you led someone to accept Jesus Christ as his or her personal Savior?" Or, "When was the last time your local church corporately fasted and prayed about the lost souls in your community?" (You may want to re-read the previous paragraph listing the nineteen characteristics that would mark the heart of people during this final period of human history.)

We cannot any longer be passive about our faith and the state of our local churches. We can no longer be passive about living Christ-like lives before a lost and dying world. Paul encouraged Timothy not to waver. Why did Paul do this? If we stop listening to truth, we risk our eternal security!

> 1 Timothy 4:1
>
> "Now the Spirit speaketh expressly, that in the latter times *some shall depart from the faith*, giving heed to seducing spirits, and doctrines of devils." (KJV, italics added)

> 2 Timothy 4:3
>
> "For the time will come when people *will not put up with sound doctrine.* Instead, to suit their own desires, *they will gather around them a great number of teachers to say what their itching ears want to hear.*" (NIV, italics added)

We are in the "latter times." Regardless of your theology or eschatology, as we just read, the Bible does say that "some shall depart from the faith, giving heed to seducing spirits, and doctrines of devils." This is not complicated. Take notice of the last part of Second Timothy 4:3, "they will gather around them a great number of teachers to say what their itching ears want to hear." When a local church seeks a new pastor, too often this is the unspoken directive which guides the search committee: *Pastor, preach what we want to hear; not the Word as it is written in the Bible!*

The return of the Messiah may be soon or it may take many more years. This should not be the only reason we live lives committed to our Father's will and Word. We are the salt and light of the world;

therefore, if we fail at doing our jobs, then an untold number of people will pay an eternal price!

> Matthew 5:13-16
> "You are the salt of the earth; but if the salt loses its flavor, how shall it be seasoned? It is then good for nothing but to be thrown out and trampled underfoot by men. You are the light of the world. A city that is set on a hill cannot be hidden. Nor do they light a lamp and put it under a basket, but on a lampstand, and it gives light to all who are in the house. Let your light so shine before men, that they may see your good works and glorify your Father in heaven." (NKJV)

> Proverbs 21:2
> "Every way of a man is right in his own eyes,
> But the Lord weighs the hearts." (NKJV)

Somewhere along the way, I either read or heard that "we are only as sick as the secrets we keep."[258] We need to be so objective about ourselves that we "get past self-deception and wishful thinking in order to soberly see who we really are." Earnest, fervent prayer involves a great deal in our self-examination. "It is the means by which we can get away from pretense and appeal to the LORD for help. We are to be

---

258 Source unknown.

doers of the Word, and not hearers only, since faith without works is dead and leads to self-deception."[259]

> 2 Corinthians 13:5
>
> "Examine yourselves as to whether you are in the faith. Test yourselves. Do you not know yourselves, that Jesus Christ is in you?—unless indeed you are disqualified." (NKJV)

[259] Hebrew for Christians, aaccessed December 11, 2015, http://www.hebrew4christians.com/Articles/Perilous_ Times/perilous_times.html.

BIBLIOGRAPHY

Bibles

(CBJ) The Complete Jewish Bible, Copyright © 1998 by David H. Stern and is published by Jewish New Testament Publications, Inc. All rights reserved. Used by permission.

(ESV) Scripture quotations are from The Holy Bible, English Standard Version® (ESV®), copyright © 2001 by Crossway, a publishing ministry of Good News Publishers. Used by permission. All rights reserved.

(KJV) The Holy Bible, The King James Version of the Bible was originally published in 1611.

(NASB) New American Standard Bible Copyright © 1960, 1962, 1963, 1968, 1971, 1972, 1973, 1975, 1977, 1995 by The Lockman Foundation, La Habra, Calif. All rights reserved.

(NIV) Scripture quotations taken from the THE HOLY BIBLE, NEW INTERNATIONAL VERSION®, NIV® Copyright © 1973, 1978, 1984, 2011 by Biblica, Inc. ® Used by permission. All rights reserved worldwide.

(NRSV) New Revised Standard Version Bible, copyright 1989, Division of Christian Education of the National Council of the Churches of Christ in the United States of America. Used by permission. All rights reserved. (New Revised Standard Bible Version Online)

Websites

http://www.academypublication.com

http://www.ancient-hebrew.org

https://www.astrotheme.com

https://www.biblestudytools.com

http://blogforthelordjesuscurrentevents.com

http://www.biblearchaeology.org

https://www.blueletterbible.org

https://www.catholic.com

http://catholicism.org

http://cgi.org

http://www.chabad.org

http://www.christianity.com

http://christinprophecy.org

http://www.christianitytoday.com

http://www.desiringgod.org

http:// www.differencebetween.net

https://www.dmv.org

https://www.en.oxforddictionaries.com

http://www.giveshare.org

https://www.haaretz.com

http://www.hebrew4christians.com

http://www.history.com

http://www.aish.com

http://www.jewishencyclopedia.com

http://www.jewishvirtuallibrary.org

http://www.jpatton.bellevue.edu

https://www.jw.org

http://www.lexiophiles.com

https://www.lifenews.com

https://www.merriam-webster.com

http://www.myjewishlearning.com

http://www.macmillandictionaries.com

http://www.messianicassociation.org

http://www.newworldencyclopedia.org/entry/Hebrew_Bible

https://www.onenewsnow.com

http://www.pewforum.org

http://www.richardwurmbrandbio.info

https://www.sharefaith.com

http://thewaybiblicalfellowship.com

https://www.thebibleproject.com

http://www.torahclass.com

http://www.vatican.va

http://vulgate.org

https://www.washingtonpost.com

http://www.yadvashem.org

Magazines

THE WEEK, September 8, 2017
THE WEEK, "Viewpoint", June 19, 2015
"The Voice of the Martyrs," October, 2017

Publications

A. N. Wilson, *Paul, The Mind of an Apostle* (WW Norton & Company: New York, NY, 1997)

Abraham J. Heschel, *Between God and Man* (New York, NY: Free Press Paperbacks, 1997)

Abraham J. Heschel (Author), Fritz A. Rothschild (Editor) *Between God and Man: An interpretation of Judaism from the Writings of Abraham Heschel* (New York: Free Press, 1959)

Alexander Archibald, *The Canon of the Old and New Testaments Ascertained, or the Bible Complete Without the Apocrypha and Unwritten Traditions*, (Princeton Press: New York, 1851)

Alexander Strauch, Biblical Eldership (Littleton, CO: Lewis and Roth Publishers, 1995)

Bruce M. Metzger, *The Early Versions of the New Testament*, (Clarendon Press: Oxford 1977)

Byram and Risager, *The Role of English language culture in the Omani language education system: An Ideological Perspective.* Language, Culture and Curriculum, 18 (3) 258-270. (1999, originally cited in Al-Issa, 2005 and in Journal of Language Teaching and Research, Vol. 4, No. 5, pp. 953-957, September 2013,

George W. Clark, *Notes on the Gospel of Matthew; Explanatory and Practical*, (Sheldon and Company, 1870)

Charles J. Hefele, *A History of the Councils of the Church*, 2, (Edinburgh, 1876)

Codex Justinianus 3.12.3, trans. Philip Schaff, *History of the Christian Church*, 5th ed. (New York, 1902)

David H. Stern, *Jewish New Testament Commentary* (Jewish New Testament Publications, Inc.: Clarksville, MD, 1992, 1996

E. Randolf Richards and Brandon J. O'Brien, *Misreading Scripture with Western Eyes* (Downers Grove: IVP Books, 2012)

E.W. Bullinger, *The Companion Bible* (Grand Rapids, Michigan: Zondervan Bible Publishers, 1974)

Earnest Martin, *Restoring the Original Bible*, (Ann Arbor, Michigan: ASK Publications, 1994)

Elie Wiesel, "Talking and Writing and Keeping Silent," in F.H. Littell and H.G. Locke, *German Church Struggle*, (Detroit; Wayne State University Press, 1974)

Eugene J. Fisher, Visions of the Others (Paulist Press: Mahwah, NJ, 1994)

Francis Frangipane, *Holiness, Truth and the Presence of God*: (Cedar Rapids, IA: Arrow Publications, 1986)

Greg Ogden, *The New Reformation* (Zondervan Publishing House: Grand Rapids, MI, 1990)

Geoffrey Parker, *The Thirty Years War* (New York: Routledge, 1984, 1997)

George W. Clark, *Notes on Gospel of Matthew* (Sheldon & Company: Philadelphia, PA, 1870)

George M. Lamsa, *Idioms in the Bible Explained* (Harper One: New York, 1985)

Jack Deere, *Surprised by the Power of the Spirit* (Zondervan: Grand Rapids, 1993)

Jeffrey M. Shaw, Timothy J. Demy, *War and Religion: An Encyclopedia of Faith and Conflict* (ABC-CLIO: Santa Barbara, CA, 2017)

Jerry Nelson, *Stepping Through Troubled Times*, (WestBow Press: Bloomington, IN, 2011)

Karen Louise Jolly, *Tradition & Diversity, Christianity in a World Context to 1500*, (Routedge: New York, 1997, 2015)

Kevin Howard, Marvin Rosenthal, *The Feats of the Lord* (Nashville, TN: Thomas Nelson, 1997)

Koninklijke Brill NV Leiden, *The Jewish Revolt Against Rome: Interdisciplinary Perspectives*, (IDC Publishers: The Netherlands, 2011)

James Carroll, *Constantine's Sword* (Houghton Mifflin Company: New York, 2002)

Norbert Lohfink, *The Covenant Never Revoked: Biblical Reflections on Christian-Jewish Dialogue* (Paulist Press: Mahwah, NJ, 1991)

Michael S. Heiser, *The Unseen Realm*, (Lexham Press: Bellingham, WA, 2015),

Michael W. Reilly, *The Journey from Darkness to Light* (Createspace Independent Publishing; Middletown, DE, 2017)

Michael W. Reilly, The Master's Model, (Columbia: Create Space Publishing, 2016)

Parker, Derek and Julia, 1983. *A history of Astrology* (Harper Collins Distribution Services: Deutsch, 1983)

Peter H. Wilson, *Europe's Tragedy: A New History of the Thirty Years War* (London: Penguin, 2010)

Rabbi Wayne Dosick, *Living Judaism* (Harper Collins: San Francisco, CA, 1995)

Shubert Spero, Holocaust and Return to Zion: A Study in Jewish Philosophy of History (Hoboken: KTAV Publishing House, Inc., 2000)

Susannah Heschel, *Abraham Geiger and the Jewish Jesus*, (The University of Chicago Press: Chicago, IL, 1998)

W. H. C. Frend, *The Rise of Christianity* (Fortress Press: Philadelphia, PA, 1984)

INDEX

1

2

A

B

C

D

E

F

G

H

I

J

K

L

M

N

O

P

Q

R

S

T

V

W

Y

Z

Made in the USA
Columbia, SC
13 August 2018